# Group Analytic Psychotherapy

Group analytic psychotherapy is internationally recognized as an effective treatment for people struggling with mental distress, personal development and interpersonal problems. Integrating psychoanalytic and social psychological thinking, and providing a group setting for self-discovery and developing social skills, long- and short-term courses in this type of therapy are increasing in popularity.

This book provides a detailed description of both long- and short-term versions of group analytic therapy, with rich and vivid clinical examples to illustrate theory and techniques. *Group Analytic Psychotherapy* describes in detail what a participant may expect, differences between short- and long-term therapy and how to behave as a group member, as well as the main issues the clinician has to deal with. Topics covered include:

- group analytic theory
- methodology
- clinical examples
- therapist adherence and competence.

Providing a basis for understanding the dynamics of groups that offer emotional support and a positive atmosphere, *Group Analytic Psychotherapy* is ideal for clinicians, students and informed patients as well as all psychodynamically oriented professionals in the field. It is an essential manual for those looking to learn the main attributes of group intervention.

**Steinar Lorentzen** is a trained psychiatrist, psychoanalyst and group analyst and a founding member of the Institute of Group Analysis, Norway. He is also Professor of Psychiatry at the University of Oslo.

# Group Analytic Psychotherapy

## Working with affective, anxiety and personality disorders

Steinar Lorentzen

Routledge
Taylor & Francis Group

LONDON AND NEW YORK

First published 2014
by Routledge
4 Park Square, Milton Park, Abingdon, Oxon OX14 4RN
605 Third Avenue, New York, NY 10017

*Routledge is an imprint of the Taylor & Francis Group, an informa business*

*British Library Cataloguing in Publication Data*
A catalogue record for this book is available from the British Library

*Library of Congress Cataloging in Publication Data*
Lorentzen, Steinar.
   Group analytic psychotherapy : working with affective, anxiety and
   personality disorder / Steinar Lorentzen.
      pages cm
   Includes bibliographical references and index.
   ISBN 978-0-415-83148-2 (hardback)—ISBN 978-0-415-83149-9 (pbk.)—
   ISBN 978-0-203-79688-7 (ebook)   1. Group psychoanalysis.   2. Group
   psychotherapy.   3. Affective disorders—Treatment.   4. Anxiety disorders—
   Treatment.   5. Personality disorders—Treatment.   I. Title.
   RC510.L67 2013
   616.89'152—dc23

                                                                2013005199


ISBN: 978-0-415-83148-2 (hbk)
ISBN: 978-0-415-83149-9 (pbk)
ISBN: 978-0-203-79688-7 (ebk)


Typeset in Garamond
by RefineCatch Limited, Bungay, Suffolk

# Contents

# Foreword

*Molyn Leszcz*

Steinar Lorentzen makes a contribution of great value to the practice of contemporary group psychotherapy in his manual: *Group Analytic Psychotherapy: Working with Affective, Anxiety and Personalilty Disorders*. This book is an important advance in addressing the important challenges which the field of group psychotherapy and group analysis must confront with regard to working within an evidence-based practice framework. It is essential in so doing that the field synthesizes both the science and art of psychotherapy. This important bridge between science and art has often fallen short, leaving the broader field polarized between clinicians on the one side and researchers on the other. Dr. Lorentzen is both an outstanding clinician and an outstanding scientist-researcher and brings that expertise to bear in this manual.

Group analysis and group analytic psychotherapy are widely practised in particular in the European context. In the hands of its practitioners it is viewed as an effective treatment and broadly accepted by patients as well. Dating back to its early origins there has been a certain resistance to the application of research methodology to the clinical field for fear of contaminating the clinical substrate by the research methodology. It is essential, however, that we as a field overcome this antipathy towards research and more rigorous evaluation if we are to continue to be an important pillar in mental health treatment in a world that demands accountability and evidence.

The development of this manual, which synthesizes the important historical work of Foulkes in the area of group analysis and contemporary developments in the field of group psychotherapy along with important contributions from the clinical research of Dr. Lorentzen and colleagues, addresses an important component of practising in an evidence-based fashion. Dr. Lorentzen's integration of clinical and research expertise challenges the misconception that our field lacks empirical evidence as demonstrated by his work in the Short- and Long-Term Group Analytic Psychotherapy (SALT-GAP) randomized controlled trial comparing these two treatments. This trial is a comparison of group therapy of 20 sessions duration versus 80 sessions in the treatment of 148 prototypical patients presenting with depression, anxiety and mild to moderate personality disorders, a highly representative clinical sample which adds to the utility of this manual. Nine therapists were trained and supervised and monitored with fidelity checks, and the manual includes the evaluation of fidelity and the competent application of the group analytic techniques. It emphasizes a form of group therapy that uses the group as an agent for change – analysis carried out in the group by the group and of the group.

It is becoming more and more recognized that evidence-based practice includes empirically supported therapies but also includes the use of clinical practice guidelines (Bernard *et al.*, 2008) and patient-centred tracking for the compiling of practice-based evidence. The use of the manual as designed by Lorentzen is very much allied with the clinical practice guidelines approach to evidence-based practice. The use of such manuals is more engaging and hopefully acceptable to practitioners than the more rigid and narrow view that evidence-based practice is restricted only to empirically supported therapies that meet rigorous standards of randomized controlled trials and replication. The intent of clinical practice guidelines or manuals such as this is to influence and inform practitioners and in so doing to increase the likelihood that participants in psychotherapy will receive a similar kind of treatment in the hands of a range of different practitioners. It is intended to supplement rather than supplant clinical judgement and, unlike other manuals that may dictate 'this is what the therapist does in session 1 and this is what the therapist does in session 2', it is more in the spirit of the manual, for example, for supportive expressive group therapy that David Spiegel and colleagues (Spiegel and Classen, 2000) constructed in a series of research trials looking at supportive expressive group therapy in the treatment of women with breast cancer. It is less prescriptive and focuses more on the gestalt of treatment and is truly dynamic in the sense of mapping out clinical theory, clinical interventions using clinical illustrations and evidence from the psychotherapy literature to articulate a substantive and reliable base for the practice of group therapy. Manuals such as this reduce the idiosyncratic application of a therapeutic model, either at the hands of an exemplary and outstanding group therapist whose work cannot be replicated by others, or by someone who practises in their own interpretation of the field without attention to the science of our work.

This manual is well written, thoughtful and provides excellent illustrations of clinical interventions. It follows important principles of fidelity in psychotherapy by articulating what interventions are essential and unique; what interventions are essential but not unique; what interventions may be utilized but are not essential nor unique; and, also proscribes interventions that would interfere with the application of the group analytic model (Waltz *et al.*, 1993). This manual will be of use both to therapists in training and to more experienced therapists to help remind them of the risk of therapeutic drift and moving away from a more rigorous application of technique influenced by counter-transference or other attenuating factors.

This manual will also be of great utility to prospective patients. There is abundant evidence that more informed participants in treatment, in particular where there is convergence with regard to patient and therapist expectancies, strengthens the therapeutic alliance which in turn improves clinical outcomes. We are dealing evermore with a patient base who truly want to make informed choices with regard to consent for treatment. This readable and accessible manual will help achieve that goal as well.

The fidelity measurements demonstrated that the group leaders were both adherent and competent in their administration of group analysis. Therapist competence was equal in both formats ranging from moderate to high, and there were no differences in therapeutic alliance or group cohesion. As anticipated and hoped, the short-term group work involved more work on circumscribed problem foci and a greater emphasis within the here-and-now, as suggested in the treatment manual. Interestingly, the level of therapist activity was equal in both the short-term and long-term groups modified by the prior findings.

My experience as a supervisor of group therapy trainees for many years has crystallized the clear impression that trainees hunger for interventions illustrated to them that are embedded in theory that is clear and robust. This is an important developmental step for them as they embark upon developing their own personal style. Until they achieve that, they want to learn, like surgical trainees, from experienced and effective practitioners with regard to technique and the rationale guiding that technique, underscoring the key principles throughout.

Particular areas that will be of use to readers include guidelines for the therapeutic use of self and how essential it is for group analysts to understand their own natural impact on their patients and what they habitually bring to the clinical environment. Also of great value are the technical distinctions between leading short-term groups and long-term groups underscoring that short-term work and long-term work are likely more on a continuum of differential emphases than being two distinct models of intervention. Importance of attention to boundaries in short-term group work is beautifully illustrated by Dr. Lorentzen and relevant to all practitioners in reminding us about the essential task of focusing attention on the resistance patients may present to accessing their internal world.

Practitioners more familiar with American approaches to group psychotherapy, for example *The Theory and Practice of Group Psychotherapy* (Yalom and Leszcz, 2005), will see much constructive interface with regard to the group analytic emphasis of the interpersonal nature of contemporary psychological difficulty and the important role of the group in creating a forum for illumination, learning and repair. Differences between models have more to do with figure–ground emphases rather than with radically different applications as they relate to working in the here-and-now; the group-as-a-whole, and the interface of here-and-now versus then-and-there foci that must be held in mind.

This manual also strikes a very important tone that may be part of the hidden curriculum in education and training of therapists. It is evident in Dr. Lorentzen's clinical illustrations and his style of writing and presentation. At the heart of this work is the delicate balance that effective group therapists must maintain between the dualities of assertion and humility, recognizing the limits of our knowledge and the hazards of blind spots while yet being persistent in being willing to open up, explore and investigate, working at various levels of inference captured well in Dr. Lorentzen's distinction between open and guided facilitation – again synthesizing the art and science of group analysis.

# Acknowledgements

This manual was written for a specific research project of short- and long-term group analytic psychotherapy (SALT-GAP) which was planned and developed during 2004–2005 and implemented during the following years. The people I want to acknowledge and thank belong to three different groups that each play a central role in carrying out all the work which leads up to this publication. My first thank you goes to the public 'Health Authority South-East' (there are four health authorities in Norway) which offered a grant in 2004–2007 which made it possible to finance this research. The Institute of Clinical Medicine, University of Oslo, as well as Oslo University Hospital, Division of Mental Health and Addiction, represent an important base for the project, and have provided practical facilities, a professional milieu and important additional economic support. The next group consists of everyone who contributed directly to the implementation of the project: first of all the group members who gave their informed consent and who contributed to the research by commenting on aspects of the treatment process and openly reporting feelings and thoughts. Their names can, of course, not be mentioned here. Next, I want to thank the local coordinators who evaluated all the patients both before therapy started and three years later, the nine therapists who each ran a short-term and a long-term group, the steering committee for the project and the two research fellows that are connected to the project: Laila Hjulstad, Knut Skjøstad, Vibeke Lohne, Allan Larsen, Kirsten Høbye, Helge Knudsen, Marthe Horneland, Dagny Sande Børnes, Ole Inge Gjøen, Wibeke Kløvning, Synnøve A. Kristiansen, Martin Mydske Nilssen, Ørjan Berg, Per Høglend, Torleif Ruud, Jan Vegard Bakali and Anette Fjeldstad. In addition, I would like to acknowledge the following institutions where the treatments were carried out: outpatient clinics at Community Mental Health Centers in Ålesund, Alna (Oslo), Sandnes and Ryfylke (Stavanger).

I want to thank the Institute of Group Analysis (IGA), London, and the Group Analytic Society (GAS), International, for economic support in the translation of these guidelines from Norwegian to English. Both organizations have also, together with the European Group Analytic Training Institutions Network (EGATIN), supported and strongly expressed the wish that these guidelines should be published. A special thank goes to Gerda Winther, the former president of GAS, who early on maintained that the publication of these guidelines would be an important contribution to the development of our group analytic field. In addition to Gerda, Chris Evans, David Kennard, Alfred Garwood, Dieter Nitzgen and Amélie Noack (all appointed by IGA, GAS or EGATIN) have been of indispensible help with theoretical, linguistic as well as practical issues concerning the publication process. I thank you all from my heart.

Last, but not least, a warm thank you goes to Ingrid, who has given support and offered important and constructive professional criticism.

Steinar Lorentzen
Oslo
May, 2013

# Abbreviations

CBT: Cognitive Behavioural Therapy
CMHC: Community Mental Health Centre
GP: General Practitioner
IPT: Interpersonal Therapy
LTG: Long-Term Group
QOR: Quality of Object Relations
RCT: Randomized Controlled Trial
SALT-GAP: Short- and Long-Term Group Analytic Psychotherapy
SD: Standard Deviation
STG: Short-Term Group

# Introduction

The empirical evidence for the general efficacy/effectiveness of group psychotherapy is substantial for a wide range of mental disorders (Fuhriman and Burlingame, 1994; Burlingame, Fuhriman, and Mosier, 2003; Burlingame, MacKenzie, and Strauss, 2004). This has been demonstrated in literature reviews and meta-analyses aggregating results from studies on different types of group psychotherapy. A main problem with the existing research is, however, that most group therapies studied are of short duration (Burlingame, Strauss, and Joyce, 2013), while longer treatments are quite common in clinical practice, at least in Europe. Another problem is that many reviews aggregate single studies of therapies with different theoretical backgrounds, which precludes the possibility of linking effect to specific theoretical concepts.

Although the number of studies is small, there are several high quality quantitative studies that have demonstrated a positive result of psycho-dynamically oriented group psychotherapy, including Group Analysis (Centre for Psychological Services Research, 2009). The few studies that demonstrate the effectiveness of *long-term* group psychotherapy (one year or longer) with outpatients are based on psychodynamic theory (e.g. Lorentzen, Bøgwald, and Høglend, 2002; Lundquist *et al.*, 2006; Lau and Kristensen, 2007; Bateman and Fonagy, 2009). This means that there is an urgent need for more research to be done.

This manual was produced for a randomized controlled trial (RCT) in group analysis/group analytic psychotherapy, called Short- and Long-Term Group Analytic Psychotherapy (SALT-GAP). The primary aim of this project is to study potential differences in outcome in short- and long-term group analytic psychotherapy. Further aims are to detect patient, therapy and therapist factors that may influence outcome and to study potential mechanisms of change. These guidelines, their theoretical underpinnings, description of therapist attitude and interventions, primarily target outpatients.

The purpose of a manual or clinical guidelines (I use these concepts interchangeably throughout this book) to be used in research is to reduce the variance in therapist activity, or to say it another way: to increase the probability that patients will be exposed to a fairly similar influence, the treatment.

Another purpose is to try to capture central aspects of the clinical phenomena through the use of theoretically relevant, standardized measures and to relate these to treatment outcome. Treatment guidelines may also be of help for trainees or more established group analysts by offering a synopsis of central aspects and a framework for the clinical essentials to be found within the rich literature of group psychotherapy. This may increase clarity and mutual understanding in the communication between professionals. According to Luborsky and Barber (1993), a treatment manual should contain an overview of interventions, clinical examples of these, and scales and measurements for checking therapy adherence and therapist competence, in order to check if the therapists deliver the prescribed treatment, and how competently they do this.

Guidelines in psychodynamic group psychotherapy, including group analysis, should not be a strait-jacket for the therapist, a recipe to be followed strictly step by step. They should include an overview of principles, aspects of methodology, suggestions for interventions and a theoretical rationale for these. My intention has been to describe two forms of dynamic group psychotherapy, one short- and one long-term (20 versus 80 weekly sessions of 90 minutes, which correspond to a treatment duration of six and 24 months, respectively). Out of considerations for the research design, the Research Steering Committee wanted the therapies to be as equal as possible, but we had, of course, to respect established knowledge about short-term therapies, which includes a need for increased therapist activity, more structuring, more focused problem area, working in the here-and-now and more attention to the termination. In addition to these 'modifications', we have described four phases in the short-term groups (MacKenzie, 1997), as a backdrop for understanding and working with the process in the short-term groups. The long-term group's guidelines build on traditional group analytic theories (Foulkes and Anthony, 1984). Although the long-term group therapy is not 'classical group analysis', if that can be said to exist in regular clinical work, we see it as close to group analysis as it is possible to come in a randomized clinical trial. The main deviations are that the therapists have not themselves evaluated the patients and composed their groups. Besides, the groups are closed with a pre-set duration. RTCs are often criticized for creating results that are irrelevant for clinicians. By including patients referred to treatment in community mental health centres (CMHC) or by private practitioners, that is psychiatrists and psychologists, we have tried to counteract some of this criticism, and maintain that our results more readily may be generalized back to a regular clinical situation. Independent coordinators who were not involved in the treatment evaluated and randomized the patients. Then the therapists met with the patients for two to four sessions before the groups started. Nine experienced therapists each conducted a short- and a long-term group of eight patients, altogether 18 groups and 148 patients.

The guidelines in this manual are an example of how *we* did it, and are not meant to be a standard for what or how it should be done, in general. Implicit in the development of guidelines for treating certain categories of patients is the conviction that group analysis is not a panacea equally effective for everyone. Each research project may have to develop their own guidelines (or manual), depending on the treatment needs of the patients under study, as well as the research questions asked. We targeted outpatients with affective (mostly depressions), anxiety and mild-to-moderate personality disorders, as we see them in our daily clinical work. Others may have wanted to do it differently, and certainly should do so, when they aim to treat patients with other disorders, like serious personality disorders, post-traumatic stress disorder, patients with addictions and eating disorders.

# Part I

# Long-term group analytic psychotherapy

# Chapter 1

# Group analytic theory

## Defining group analysis

Group analysis was developed by S. H. Foulkes. For a short biography and bibliography, see Pines (1983, pp. xi–xviii). Group analysis is a form of psychodynamic group therapy where treatment of individual patients takes place in the group and is effected by the group, including the leader. The group of people gathered is therefore the actual treatment instrument, and it is the therapist's task to involve the group in this process. Although Foulkes developed several concepts to describe the structure and process in therapeutic groups, group analysis shares many of the basic assumptions of other psychodynamic or psychoanalytic therapies: a developmental perspective on personality, existence of internal representations of interpersonal relationships, psychological causation, influence of unconscious individual and group processes on behaviour, ubiquity of psychological conflict and the existence of psychic defences.

## The objective of the therapy

Group analysis is an investigative therapy which seeks to optimize interaction between group members with a view to raising awareness of the group's dynamics and the individual member's intrapsychic conflicts, and eventually to contribute to correcting irrational forms of behaviour and problematic interactional patterns. The use of these insights and new corrective experiences to promote behaviour change within and outside the group can provide a starting point for a more realistic self-image, for changing dysfunctional interpersonal behaviour patterns and for the adoption of new, more functional ones.

## View of human nature

Foulkes emphasized that man is primarily a social being, and that individuality arose in the late stage of the industrial revolution (biologically speaking, the individual is the smallest unit, while the group is the basic psychological unit). One of his fundamental principles was that 'the whole' (the group) is more elementary than 'the parts' (the individuals). He used the term 'foundation matrix' to characterize our common cultural background (the facts that we have a body, that we are born and are socialized in a group, that we depend on communication, that we have a language, etc.). He considered this common background to be of vital importance in our being able to understand each other. Much of this background we take for granted, 'like the air we breathe in and out', without us being conscious of it.

## Mental disorders

Foulkes believed that individual psychic disorders, that is especially neuroses and personality disorders, are related to human relationships. They manifest themselves in the individual's relationship with a group and often occur or are found only in the patient's relationship with those who are nearest to him, the primary group. Since mental disorders occur in man's relationship to his surroundings, Foulkes believed that the best treatment for these disorders is group analysis, as the basis for a deeper understanding and correction of dysfunctional human relationships.

## The therapeutic group and the therapy process

The composition of the group is usually determined according to 'the Noah's Ark principle': the members should be drawn from all age groups, both sexes, the anxious–more uninhibited and extroverted–introverted spectrums, and should include at least two members from each of these groups, in order to prevent anyone feeling like an outsider. The idea is that various types of problems and personalities provide space for the softening of defences and new learning. In our research project (SALT-GAP) the therapists do not select patients and compose the groups, but the patients are randomized into groups, which will hopefully result in a roughly equal distribution with respect to sex and age, degree and type of psychopathology. Foulkes raised the question of how a group of deviant individuals could 'normalize' a person, and answered it himself by saying that 'collectively they constitute the norm from which, individually, they deviate (Foulkes, 1977, p. 297). All members are characterized by the foundation matrix, which is a given factor in the group. In addition, the group develops its own history over time. Foulkes used the image of a network, where individuals are located at the point of intersection ('nodal points') between the fibres, to describe the group. The network consists of 'all the individual mental processes, the psychological medium in which they meet, communicate, and interact' (Foulkes and Anthony, 1984, p. 26). The processes are transpersonal, i.e. they penetrate to the core of every individual. He called this network 'the dynamic matrix' or 'the interactional matrix', which is a network that is developed and shaped by the individuals in the group. He saw this term as a construct, in the same way that he saw the term 'traffic' or 'mind', and he found the term useful when it came to characterizing the 'group-as-a-whole'. By relating to each other, group members recreate the conditions from their own primary network, as they perceive them, consciously or unconsciously. Foulkes saw this as the group's equivalence to the 'transference neurosis', as can most clearly be seen in the analytic situation. In today's terminology, one would be more inclined to say that members develop multiple transferences onto other members, including the leader. These will be characterized by the attachment pattern to the primary object and more or less processed relational patterns to other members of the family group.

Foulkes saw communication as absolutely essential for *the therapeutic process*. The essence of the process is 'working towards an ever more articulate form of communication'. He believed that, while each member of the group would tend to reverberate at every group event which was consistent with the level he was at, this level and the depth of communication intent would change if group members were aware of and able to work through their problems. Foulkes used the phrase 'ego-training in action' to describe an important mechanism which would contribute to the change. This concept can be understood as follows: the patient, who will constantly be stimulated to act in the group, postpones this and discloses his problems, reflects and tries to recognize his own feelings instead. The new experience which is provided by the insight gained through analysis and new responses from others in the group will lead to the modification of the member's previous behaviour and make him open to new learning.

## Common and specific group factors

Certain common factors exist in all therapeutic groups: a sense of being supported and accepted, the opportunity to speak and be listened to, to share with others, to have the same emotional experiences as others and to cope with isolation and loneliness.

In addition, Foulkes described several group-specific factors (Foulkes and Anthony, 1984, p. 149).

### Socialization through the group

By observing how others in the group, including the leader, relate in interpersonal situations, opportunities arise for imitation and identification. The possibility of directly testing the new interpersonal strategies which the group provides represents a great opportunity for social learning.

### The mirroring phenomenon

The group situation has been likened to a hall of mirrors, where an individual is confronted with a variety of his social, psychological and physical characteristics (body image).

### The condenser phenomenon

This term has been used to describe a sudden discharge of deep and primitive material or the pooling of associated thoughts (ideas) in the group.

### The chain phenomenon

From time to time, the group comes close to free association on account of its own characteristic, free-floating discussion. This often proves to be the case in a well-established group, in the form of a chain reaction, in which each member contributes an important and idiosyncratic link to the chain.

### Resonance

Communication in the group bears the hallmarks of both 'the dynamic matrix' and 'the foundation matrix'. Whereas 'the foundation matrix' is based on a common biological and cultural background, 'the dynamic matrix' represents the 'artificially created' but potentially intimate network developed by the members of therapeutic group. All group members 'talk' and 'understand' language, but they interpret or misinterpret it in keeping with the resonance inside them, which is created through that which is referred to at any given time.

## The therapist

Foulkes downgraded the therapist's importance and called him the 'conductor'. He also compared the therapeutic group with a symphony orchestra, where one, first and foremost, experiences mental processes which take place as a united whole. However, it follows from what I have outlined in the next chapter in the 'Therapist responsibilities' section that this role, nonetheless, carries a significant responsibility. The therapist makes himself available to the group, in particular as a transference object, and he should allow himself to be led by the group. The leader is on the other side, an instrument of the group, or should be one. In return, he must follow the group's leadership, and he should not, for example, use the group as an audience. Ideally, he should leave it to the group to capture the meaning and to place the action in the appropriate dynamic setting. When this does not happen, however, he has the ultimate responsibility for doing this.

# Chapter 2

# Methodology

## General information about the group

Each group can be analyzed in terms of structure, process and content (de Maré, 1972).

### Structure

The *structure* consists of the room, the arrangement of chairs, the duration of sessions and the therapy, the timing of sessions, the frequency of sessions, the financial arrangement, as well as any rules for behaviour inside and outside the group. The main rationale for having a structure is to create a frame in which the individual members' and the group's idiosyncratic behaviour become visible. The therapist is responsible for maintaining the structure and for understanding and intervening when boundary incidents take place. The structure is also affected by the group composition and by whether the group is open or closed.

### Process

The *process* consists of communication and other interactions which develop in the course of a session, and from session to session – over time. The 'ideal goal' is to develop a working group which is characterized by being task-oriented, where all members are involved and where communication is characterized by free group association. This means the members make associations with what is going on at any time, and the group develops an increasingly investigative, personal and open tone over time. The therapist should facilitate this process with his interventions.

### Content

The *content* of a group consists of working towards a deeper understanding of statements and interactions. In this context, 'deeper' means the preconscious or unconscious meaning of what is happening, for the individual member, sub-groups of members and/or the group-as-a-whole. The therapist's task is to assist in clarifying the latent content of statements and interactions. The clarification is mainly given with respect to the here-and-now, but it may also focus on group members' history and the social unconscious.

## Therapist responsibilities

a.  To involve the group members and the group in the therapeutic process.
b.  To maintain the group's structure and to try to understand and intervene in boundary incidents.
c.  To facilitate the group process.
d.  To interpret and translate.

A key overarching responsibility which must be kept in mind during the performance of the specific tasks mentioned above is that the therapist should seek to develop an analytic culture that the other group members can become part of. His model function is crucial, because he welcomes all communication as valuable; he is non-directive, he clarifies and interprets or translates preconscious/unconscious material, in order to promote the opportunity for members to learn something new about themselves and others. It is also important that he understands his position as a transference figure and that he is willing to comment on the relationships which group members develop to him and to each other, to make them the object of analysis. This analytic approach enables him to respond appropriately to the transference reactions and everything else going on in the same spirit. In the long run, this will promote understanding and tolerance amongst the other group members, which in return will contribute to their further development.

## The contract between patient and therapist

Each patient agrees to work in a group with a therapist and six to eight other patients for a predetermined period of time, which in this case is about two years, that is altogether 80 weekly sessions, lasting 90 minutes, which take place at a fixed time. All patients are informed about the group's basic rules regarding commitment to participation and responsibilities inside and outside the group. Each session is wrapped up by the therapist at a scheduled time. The patient pays a charge for therapy by arrangement with the therapist. Patients are asked to talk freely and openly about any subject which they raise during the session. On his part, the therapist will try to help patients understand and resolve the problems which have brought them into therapy.

# Therapist interventions

In order to achieve the objective of the therapy, the patients should be encouraged to be open verbally and through interaction with other group members, including the therapist. That creates the conditions whereby common and group-specific factors can become effective, in addition to more or less patient-specific interventions from other group members, including the therapist.

An overview of the therapist's interventions is offered by Roberts (2000).

## Maintenance of structure

This includes all activity whose aim is to clarify or define a limit, which may include the place, time, membership, task or rules. This can apply to the whole group or an individual member, including the therapist.

## Open facilitation (process)

This characterizes an intervention which aims to move the group forward. It is not necessarily based on any particular interpretation or hypothesis put forward by the therapist, nor does it relate to any unconscious level of understanding.

## Guided facilitation (process)

This includes all promoting comments which are not 'open', but which show that the therapist has a hypothesis as a background for his questions, enquiries and observations.

## Interpretation (contents and form)

This consists of a verbal intervention from the therapist which puts words to feelings or meaning that is latent in the group-as-a-whole or in what individual members say or do. In group analysis, where the therapy process consists of an ever-increasing expansion and deepening of communication, the term 'translation' is often used instead of 'interpretation'. 'Translation' of behavioural and interactional events is a more tentative approach, working from 'the surface', and keeping open other possibilities for the understanding of phenomena, whilst avoiding asserting oneself as an unilateral authoritative specialist on the unconscious mental life of others, which could adversely interfere with the development of a group-analytic culture. However, situations may arise where it is important to take responsibility and to be clear when one feels sure about a particular situation. Autonomy and natural self-assertion is also part of the group-analytic culture.

## No immediate response

This intervention reflects the fact that much of the therapist's behaviour consists of silent observation of the group. Depending on the situation in the group, the therapist will sometimes refrain from saying or doing anything whilst reserving the right to intervene at a later stage, depending on the group's further development.

## Action

Action covers all physical activity which the therapist might undertake in the group, for example, leaving his chair to close the window or touching another group member.

## Self-disclosure

This is any statement by the therapist about the content of his internal world, thoughts or feelings, or the external world, which does not fit into any of the other categories.

## Modelling

Modelling consists of all behaviours which the therapist carries out with the implicit intention that they be adopted and become part of the group's or members' repertoire. This includes, for example, mastering stressful events or unpleasant social situations, or modelling an analytic enquiring and compassionate attitude.

# Therapist attitude

The therapist's influence consists both of how he behaves and who he is, of his attitude as well as what he says and does. In group analysis, as in all other treatments working with transference, it is therefore important to know something about what impact one has on others.

In order to facilitate group process, the therapist, in his approach, should strive to:

1.  Maintain an expectation that patients should speak and get involved in what others are saying or doing. Members of such a group become active participants, not passive recipients of the treatment. They are at the heart of the group and are continually confronted with situations which they have to tackle actively, which is in itself an exercise in mastering interpersonal relationships.

2.  Encourage patients to put aside self-criticism. This can be done by telling them that they are expected to communicate what they are thinking and that they should say things as and when they crop up. One might need to emphasize that a therapy group is different from an ordinary social situation in this particular respect.

3.  Encourage patients to explore aspects of themselves and the group, including their own and others' unpleasant feelings. By accepting and encouraging statements which would not normally be tolerated in an ordinary social situation, the therapist shows that direct communication of personal feelings and experiences is desirable.

4.  Use the group situation to actively demonstrate that interaction is a place where subjective worlds meet, where everyone may have something to learn. A statement which one member addresses to another at an early stage in the process will often have a strongly projectional stamp, and contain more of the commentator's subjective world than of a more 'objective' reality. All statements are important, nonetheless.

5.  Show interest in the patients' subjective impression of the therapist and of other group members.

6.  Chart links between the patient's relationships with other people in his life and his relationship with the therapist and other group members.

7.  An important dimension of all psychodynamic therapy is the extent to which the therapist should strike a balance between narratives, which patients bring to the group dealing with other people in the present or the past, and the material which is activated in the group, through interaction between members. Many are of the view that it can be important to keep the focus on patients and their relationship to the therapist in the here-and-now in the treatment situation, rather than on the patient and his significant others *outside* the treatment situation in the there-and-then. This does not apply unconditionally, especially if patients associate to their other present or past relationships based on what happens in the group. That, in fact, creates the basis for emotional learning and understanding. Nor does it apply when patients bring to the group emotionally loaded, fresh events which are greatly preoccupying them. Such events often provide good learning opportunities for them and for others, while the emotionality at the same time 'awakens' the group. However, many may have stereotypical, long and intellectual explanations about why things are the way they are, or they bring up an ongoing external relationship when the atmosphere in the group becomes uncomfortable. Then a gentle intervention may be appropriate. An example is: 'It seems to me that you have told this story many times before without it having apparently helped you to move on. I think it would be very interesting if you could tell us when you experience something similar here, so we can look into it.' Or, in the latter case: 'Did

you notice that, when it was getting a bit tense between you and NN, you started talking about . . .?'

In concluding this section we would specifically emphasize the importance of the three essential methodological 'measures' in group analysis discussed above and in several other places in the guidelines. They come under the headings of both the therapist's interventions and his attitude, and may therefore be difficult to unambiguously classify: (i) the development of a group analytic culture; (ii) switching the focus in the group between here-and-now and there-and-then; (iii) executing a careful balance between interpretation and translation.

# Chapter 3

# Technique

## Preparation of patients

The 'negotiations' around a treatment contract will include different aspects of group participation. Patients are informed about group size and composition, time, location, duration, price, rules, etc. It may be important to help patients understand that the group is a place especially suited for working on interpersonal problems. If the patient is unaware of these aspects of his or her problems, it can be important to try to reformulate the problems in an interpersonal language. It is also important to discuss their goal(s) for the therapy. The therapist also has a responsibility of informing patients about the purpose of the group, what is expected of them and something of how they have to behave in the group. Rules about openness, activity, duty of not revealing things outside the group, etc., should not be presented in an authoritarian way, since the therapist aims from the start to build an accepting and caring group culture, based on equality. It may also be important to say something about previous positive experiences with group therapy, what group research results show, and so forth, in order to create positive expectations for the therapy. This motivational work may be especially important because patients are often less motivated for group therapy than individual therapy. A primary reason for this might be that just the thought of having to relate to several persons at the same time mobilizes anxiety and resistance. This is easy to understand since interpersonal problems are often central elements in the cluster of problems patients face. This affords us the opportunity to demonstrate and explore with the patient what their anxiety and scepticism is about. As a consequence of this it may be possible, even in the preparatory sessions, to formulate central issues that need to be dealt with and worked through, for example the wish to be 'the only one', fear of being dominated or of dominating others, fear of becoming everyone's helper, fear of hurting others, etc. It is especially important to explore all negative ideas and expectations, which, if not addressed, may easily lead to destructive acting out.

## Guidelines for interventions

The therapist's activities consist of *observation*, *reflection* and *intervention*, which can either take place sequentially or overlap each other.

### Observation

The therapist should focus on the overall interactional field by adopting a position similar to that which Freud recommended for psychoanalysis: namely, free-floating attention. However, in this particular case, we are dealing with the group-as-a-whole. During this process, the therapist will constantly find that particular individuals, statements, interactions, emotions, etc., are coming to the fore of what he or she is observing. What is in the foreground may be in a constant state of flux, but it is also possible that some things will remain in the foreground for a lengthy period of time. The background is made up of the group-as-a-whole and, in addition to the here-and-now interaction, it includes both the *history* and the *context*.

However, even if the therapist focuses on the whole group, it is important to underline that he or she must have a 'bifocal' orientation, towards both the individual and the group. They carry with them both the group's and all the group members' history, the biographical content as they have presented it and that which has been created through their participation in the group. The group's history is *distinctive* for each individual group, because it is formed by the specific individuals who constitute the group. In this context, *contextual* means both the physical setting, for example whether the group meets in a hospital, private office or an outpatients' clinic, but also prominent current phenomena which are affecting the group at that time. Examples of this are absence of individual group members, if it is the last meeting before the holidays, noise from the street, whether or not it is the day when the session fees are due, etc.

The theory of the individual as a nodal point in an interactional network is important in planning the therapist's interventions. In a therapeutic group one often speaks of the individual as being a disturbing point in the pathogenic network. A key prerequisite for understanding and interventions are the questions of *configuration* (pattern) and *localization*.

- *Configuration*: Based on observations of therapeutic groups, one can deduce the principle that every event in a group, even if it apparently involves only one or two members, is part of a configuration which involves the group-as-a-whole. This event is part of a Gestalt configuration or pattern and constitutes 'the figure' or the foreground, while 'the ground' or background manifests itself in the rest of the group.
- *Localization*: This relates to 'the cause' of the disturbance.

These points will be explained in greater detail below, in the clinical examples on interpreting.

## Reflection

Roberts (2000) recommend the following sequence when considering any intervention.

### What is the situation in the group?

The situation is assessed on the basis of activity levels, emotionality and topic. Are most or all of the members active or is there one that speaks all of the time? Does the activity consist of interaction or do they all speak at once? Are the others attentive or is there anyone who seems to be uninterested or distant? What kinds of feelings are prominent in the group? Is everyone focused on a single topic, has the group been discussing a limited number of topics or is it impossible to identify any particular topic at all? Do the members seem interested in what they are talking about, are they presenting emotionally loaded personal material or are they involved in intellectual deliberations?

### What processes contribute to it?

Had the group already started discussing certain topics in the waiting room which they then continued to discuss during the session? Did anything special happen in the group last time which was carried over into today's session in one form or another, including silence? Did a member get the ball rolling with something important that had happened or that he had thought about since the last session? Are the other members freely associating with this or are they sitting in silence and listening, possibly for fear of interrupting? Can repetitive patterns be observed in any of the individuals as an expression of the conflicts they are carrying inside?

### What are they not speaking about?

Often, a group will decide not to comment on important events in the group: for example, the fact that someone is missing, that something important happened in the previous session, that the therapist has been unempathic, etc. It is important that the therapist is alert to this, because the 'silence' is often neurotically motivated, because they feel an obligation to spare each other's feelings, they are afraid of expressing irritation, of hurting others or of incurring the anger of others, etc.

### Is the situation constructive, destructive or neutral?

Is the group blocked or is it moving in a positive direction? Is anyone being attacked or placed in a scapegoat role? Is anyone being abused in some other way, for example, by being interviewed in an unempathic fashion, more reminiscent of an interrogation?

### Is it desirable to change the situation?

If no one in the group intervenes when the group is blocked or keeps going round in circles, if someone is being attacked or abused, if the silence is long and unproductive, or if the group is struggling to understand the process and has almost reached the goal, the answer is 'yes'.

### Is it possible to change it?

If the answer is 'no', one can either wait until one considers it possible, or one can share one's helplessness with the group.

### What interventions could affect the situation and the processes which are contributing to it?

Everything that is said in a group will to varying degrees be important to other members. However, the therapist should try to think through possible consequences of addressing the whole group, certain sub-groups or individual group members, or possibly all the elements. If the issue at stake is resistance, one can describe or interpret it in terms of content and form, at the level one thinks will give the greatest chance of success. The same goes for helping individual group members to grasp the meaning of the group's configuration and the underlying driving forces, the localization.

### Do I have the necessary intervention in my repertoire?

Hopefully you do, otherwise you can ask the group.

### Is the time ripe for an intervention?

The question of the right timing applies to both an assessment of the receptivity in the group-as-a-whole, sub-groups and individual members. Are configurations and possibly the localization clear enough to enable others to understand what is meant by the intervention? If not, an intervention will, in the best-case scenario, 'fall on stony ground', but it may also result in an enhanced defence. When dealing with resistance, possibly related to dysfunctional character traits in an individual member, it is important that the therapist's comment is not perceived as a serious narcissistic attack. This makes the way interventions are formulated important. It is also necessary that a good rapport with the patient is developed. Cohesion in the group should also be good before one interprets, which means that, in the early phase, the therapist should mainly stick to structure maintaining and facilitating interventions.

### Intervention

Much of the therapist's time is spent listening, observing and reflecting. This precedes intervention or interpretation, for that matter. In group analytic long-term therapy the therapist's main role is a reflecting one, which is a necessary prerequisite for any intervention. The therapist uses his observations, the foreground and background, the experience of the individuals or the group, including any knowledge the therapist has of their history. The therapist observes emotionality, the distribution of affects, the words used, topics, similarities and differences, the way things are expressed. He or she uses their experience, what they have read or experienced in their own group therapy or other groups, and what they know about unconscious processes. Secondly, the therapist takes into account contextual factors. Is anyone missing? Do we have any new members? Has the therapist or anyone else been ill and did anything happen in the last session which may have caused a strong reaction in someone?

An important overriding principle is that the therapist should leave it to the group to resolve as many issues as possible. If the group is working well, the therapist should keep quiet, because the group is the instrument he or she uses, whenever possible. Ideally, the group's role is to capture the meaning and to place that which is happening in an appropriate dynamic setting. At the same time, one should bear in mind that the therapist has *the main responsibility* for creating and maintaining a group analytic situation, i.e. an atmosphere that provides the optimal conditions for reaching the objectives of the therapy. This includes mobilizing therapeutic potentials and translating or interpreting what happens in the group, thereby promoting change in the patients, and the leader. He or she should only intervene when the group becomes unproductive.

## Examples of different types of interventions

### Maintenance of structure

'Attacks' on the group structure, so-called boundary incidents, may take the form of lateness, patients missing a session because they have had 'a bad day', failure to pay the session fees, breach of confidentiality or of the rule that patients must not meet up outside the group, refusal to disclose personal problems, lack of commitment to others, destructive attacks on fellow patients or breach of contract, eating and drinking during group meetings, arbitrary use of group meetings as a discussion or 'chat forum', etc.

These events are important for the following reasons:

- They are often a cover for important thoughts and feelings, frequently negative, which must be clarified to enable the individuals or the group to develop further.
- In their efforts to build a group analytic culture, members must be made aware of their own and others' internal world. This requires that the therapist and other group members take these incidents seriously.
- Negative transference might build up and lead to acting out outside the group, possibly in the form of someone dropping out.
- The group structure is one of the therapist's most valuable 'tools'. Indifference to or failing to pick up on these events or take them seriously, suggests, at best, the acting out of counter-transference by the therapist, or at worst, that he lacks confidence in his own methodology. Both are harmful to the patients and the group.

The therapist should, as far as possible, avoid referring to rules. Initially, any boundary incident should be addressed. If someone avoids commenting on their absence or late arrival, one could ask them what had happened. The third time someone arrives late because of 'heavy traffic' or 'because they *had* to finish something at work', the evidence indicates that the behaviour signals something about them as a person and/or their relationship with the group. The same applies to the third time a person fails to bring their money, fails to call or to cancel their attendance at a session, etc. Some may, for instance, keep on forgetting that they were meant to be in the group at a certain time, and will consistently insist, without having met any critical voice, that they feel comfortable with and like to be working in a group. One can then ask when the last occasion was they could remember when they thought about the group, how they felt when they discovered they had forgotten about it, how they thought the reactions of others would be, and if they saw anything particular in their mind's eye, etc. One could also ask whether the same phenomenon often manifests itself in other situations. Some members sometimes perceive this as moralizing and scolding, rather than an attempt to understand what is happening inside them. Usually, someone in the group gets the point and steps in to help. The precondition is, of course, that the therapist does not get *too* irritated about what has happened.

There is important information about personality and current relationships hidden in the boundary incident. By questioning like this, it may become possible to tease out more details. Some have a tendency to do things out of routine or duty, suppress negative feelings, be afraid that others might think they are negative, etc. By questioning, the therapist models a group analytic approach.

The fourth time someone forgets to bring the fee and says 'if you absolutely have to have it, I can go to a cashpoint and get it for you (you moneygrubber!)', the therapist should say 'Yes, please', whether he or she needs the money at that moment or not. In that way, they give the patient an opportunity to connect with the feelings which are being acted out and thereby bringing them into the group. Almost without exception, such incidents strengthen the alliance and increase group cohesion, if the ability and willingness for growth are there. An example: one patient who had been in the group for six months told the therapist he might have to leave the group after that session, because he had decided to move 500 kilometres away. If it was necessary, he could travel back every week to continue with the group (the therapist found himself thinking about how the patient projected his own need for more treatment in this group, onto someone else. He also considered that the patient's willingness to travel so far sounded like a penitential exercise). The patient also thought that he might be able to find a group in his new place, and then resume group sessions in his present group when he moved back in six months' time. The group and the therapist quickly realized that travelling 500 kilometres each way would be unrealistic and that, by choosing to move, he had abruptly ended the treatment in a way which was unfortunate for him as well as the group. He had made the decision without discussing it in the group, which was a repetition of similar impulsive 'choices' he had made in his past. During the rest of the session he demonstrated his reluctance to take the responsibility for his own treatment, and his unrealistic expectations about what therapy could do for him and his tendency of devaluating the importance of relationships also became clearer.

A woman in the same group addressed the therapist after a session and told him that she also was going to terminate therapy. During the preceding session she had asked what 'exposure therapy' was, and after the therapist had explained that, she said she thought it might be something that would be helpful for her. The therapist mentioned this incident during the subsequent session, having first waited a while for her to bring it up. She insisted that she was feeling a lot better now and that she would either get along fine without therapy or try something else. The group spent the whole session investigating what she had learned, and what remained to be worked with. It eventually became clear that her desire to stop coming was an acting out of anger about not having been given enough of a chance in the previous session. This anger had taken the form of the same self-destructiveness that had often played itself out in her other relationships. Her understanding of this enabled her to continue.

## Open and guided facilitation

Open and guided facilitation, both of which are interventions aimed at facilitating a process, differ from each other, depending on whether or not the therapist has a hypothesis about what is happening as the basis for his or her comment. Both interventions are used 'to help the group move on' when it is going round in circles, when it has ground to a halt or when it has otherwise become unproductive. An example is when members keep on bickering, get hung up on semantic subtleties, technical and practical tasks, etc. Comments such as: 'I wonder what is going on here now', 'what is all this bickering about?', 'I wonder what those of you who are keeping quiet are feeling' are examples of open facilitation. Comments such as: 'I wonder if this bickering is a reflection of a number of you actually being unhappy with me or the group' or 'I am getting the sense that this overwhelming preoccupation with what words really mean might be a manifestation of your desire that I should give clearer instructions about how you should relate to each other in the group' suggest that the therapist has a hypothesis about what lies behind the observed phenomena. The first type of intervention leads, at best, to the other group members also starting to share the therapist's curiosity about what is happening, and in the worst case, the therapist continuing to puzzle about the situation, while the group carries on as before. Guided facilitation leads, at best, to the group grinding to a halt, beginning to question or, often, to someone responding with a question: 'What do you mean?' In such a case, the therapist can share parts of his or her hypothesis and the group can move on. At worst, the group carries on doing what it was doing or belittles the therapist's hypothesis. Nevertheless, the therapist has got something new to think about.

### No immediate response

This form of intervention may be necessary when the therapist does not know what to say or when he or she is unsure what would actually be helpful. Often, there will be a controlled silence, as a result of the therapist wanting to hear what the other group members have to say.

### Action

In a group analytic situation this could mean passing the tissues if one of the members starts crying, allowing trips to the toilet now and then, if necessary and this being to both the therapist's and the group's benefit, switching on the answering machine if this is not already done when the phone happens to ring, opening or closing the window if the temperature is above 30 centigrades (this should not be interpreted as an expression of unconscious wishes, but rather be praised as a 'life-saving favour' carried out by one group member), or leaving the room if the fire alarm goes off. Any patient who wants to leave the room should be allowed to do so, unless it is necessary to retain the patient in order to prevent an impending disaster, like for example suicide.

### Self-disclosure

The therapist should disclose as few details about his or her private life as possible and only if asked to do so, like if they are married, have children or what they are going to do on holiday, etc. The therapist should ask members what they have imagined before or, sometimes better, after he or she has answered. Often, however, the therapist is asked what he or she is thinking, either at times when he fails to give 'an immediate response' or if someone has shared a problem with the group. In the first case, the therapist may sometimes share his surprise, uncertainty or tentative hypotheses about what this might be about, or he could do his best to try to formulate an answer which will stimulate the analytic process in the group.

Examples: After a long silence, the therapist is asked why he has not said anything. He answered, truthfully, that he felt he had run out of ideas and was wondering if it was just him or whether others also felt the same. Or: 'I am thinking about this silence and trying to understand what it means'. If there are questions about specific problems related to marriage, inheritance, children, etc., the therapist could avoid answering them directly by putting them out to the group, saying: 'Some of you here might have experience in this area?' Or he could dodge the question and address the affect in question, like the desire to receive help, for someone to remove a burden from the patient, how unfair things can be, or how other people can be perceived as unpleasant. At such times, the therapist should give his or her professional opinion, but should try to do so in a 'Socratic way': if a patient is faced with an existential choice, such as we all are facing at times or have faced in the past, he could outline the options based on his knowledge of the patient. But if the choice is a neurotic one, like the expression of a patient's repetitive, destructive patterns, this should be pointed out.

For example: 'From the way that you have described her, I am getting the sense that this person is a carbon copy of your ex-wife. I cannot quite grasp, though, what traits she has that you said previously you were looking for in a woman'. Or: 'I think you should think twice before you ditch this friend. I realize you have been hurt but, on the other hand, you do not have that many friends, and I guess the actual question is whether "the perfect friend" really exists. Let us, instead, look at what lies behind your strong reaction to people sometimes wanting to keep themselves to themselves'.

### Modelling

Everything the therapist says in a group takes on extra meaning and is something that others can easily latch on to. Just as in individual therapy, patients in group therapy should internalize the therapist and the group, so that, in the long run, they are able to continue the analysis on their own. We also want them to internalize the therapist's and the group's supportive and controlling role, the superego. This will be useful for both neurotics, who, strictly speaking, have an overactive superego, and patients with certain personality disorders, who may have a defective or rudimentary superego. This also says something about the need to work individually with patients in a group, too.

## Interpretations

Interpretations are traditionally regarded as the most important intervention in psychoanalysis. In this regard, it might be of interest to mention that recent research (Høglend *et al.*, 2006) has shown that, in short-term individual therapy, interpretations are more effective for patients with relatively poor scores on the quality of object relations (QOR) scale than for those with higher scores. This may seem to run counter to what traditionally has been seen as a sign of suitability for psychoanalysis, namely that patients have a relatively well-integrated personality structure.

In group analysis, there has been less unanimity, at least in relation to using traditional individual interpretations of impulse and defence in the transference, both in the group, in relation to the patient's relationships outside therapy or in a historical context, like significant others in childhood. Foulkes believed that the actual therapy process consisted of an expanding and deepening of the communication process. He has described this on several occasions (e.g. Foulkes, 1977, p. 112). Given the orthodox Freudian training he had, however, it is likely that he worked very intensively with individual patients in the group, which has also been confirmed by people who saw him work (personal communication, Malcolm Pines). There is also evidence which suggests that Foulkes quite actively intervened in his groups, perhaps contradicting his own point about handing over most of the therapy to the group. In this way he was one of many analysts of his time who were seen as 'established authorities' on the unconscious. It is also plausible that his attitude gradually changed before and while he moved towards group analysis. In line with group analytic theory, many group analysts prefer to speak of 'translation', rather than 'interpretation', when they are addressing manifest behaviour and statements, attributing them to an underlying or deeper meaning. The dangers of being too withholding may be that the therapist denies the importance of his own experience, and that statements become too vague or imprecise, and therefore difficult to take a stance on. The therapist could also model an 'everything is just fine' attitude, which may be at odds with the climate of respect and egalitarianism that he or she wants to cultivate. To avoid this he or she could therefore favour that interpretations, as opposed to facilitating or modelling interventions, should be presented in a fairly articulate language. There must, of course, also be an awareness that this is one of many possible formulations, that it is the *therapist's* formulation and that it may also be coloured by the therapist's counter-transference and personality, not only his or her knowledge and expertise. The interpretation may focus on a single individual, on the interaction between individuals, on both the individual and the group, on a sub-group or on the group-as-a-whole. Some examples of all these forms of interpretation will be presented in Chapters 4 and 8.

## The dimension of support – activation (challenge)

It is both impossible and futile to try to prescribe how the therapist should behave in all situations. The idea behind this dimension is that the therapist's approach may be more or less challenging and anxiety-provoking. Also, his attitude and interventions may be graded according to a scale from 'very supportive' to very 'activating'. MacKenzie (1997) equals 'very activating' to being very interpretative, but here it is used in a wider sense (see below). The therapist has to, at any time, adapt himself to the patients' and the group's needs. These needs depend on what problems the patients have, the stage in the development of the group, as well as variations in anxiety level, generated within a single session. Degree of cohesion and therapeutic alliance are important hallmarks. The question is: what kind of mixture of support and activating strategies are most useful in a given situation?

The therapist's interventions should ideally lead to an increase in cooperation, positive alliance and cohesion in the group. Short-term groups do not offer opportunity for extensive repairs of the therapeutic alliance, which may make this dimension slightly more important in STG (short-term groups) than in LTG (long-term groups).

Some research indicates that supportive techniques are also important factors in the treatment of better-integrated patients. In order to differentiate between more supportive and a more activating interpretative therapy, we will include some slightly reworked points from MacKenzie (1997).

1.  The therapeutic alliance is important in both supportive and more interpretative therapies.
2.  Technical neutrality: in the supportive model the therapist is more transparent and feels free to express acceptance, respect and liking for the patient. In the interpretative model the therapist will only deviate from technical neutrality as much as is needed to preserve the therapeutic alliance.
3.  Therapist attitude or style: in the supportive model the therapist is more conversational. The therapist should be professional, but to a larger degree focused on 'the real relationship'. Longer silences and lack of answers to the patients' questions are banned. In the interpretative model the therapist is less transparent.
4.  Goal-directedness: in the supportive model the conversation is goal-directed. In the interpretative model the therapist encourages free-floating associations and there is no planned theme.
5.  Therapeutic focus: in the supportive model the therapist seeks to identify and describe patterns on a behavioural, cognitive or interpersonal level in order to modify it. In the interpretative model the therapist to a larger extent emphasizes affective aspects and interpretations that seek to

connect intrapsychic conflicts between wishes and motives with present anxiety and earlier experiences. Underlining progress or improvement, and the instillation of hope and praise, may be used more in the supportive model. In the interpretative model the self-esteem is expected to improve as a consequence of better functioning and insight.

6.  Handling anxiety: in the supportive model one tries to avoid therapy-related anxiety and to pick it up immediately if it appears as a side effect of the work in the group. In the interpretative model it is expected that therapy-related anxiety may increase as a consequence of the therapist's more expectant attitude. It is only addressed directly if it becomes destructive.

7.  Handling defence: in the supportive model the defences are to a larger degree left alone, unless they are eminently immature and destructive. In the interpretative model it is a goal to understand defences and why they are needed.

8.  Therapist techniques: focusing, reframing, clarifications and confrontations, as well as challenging, are used in both models. In the supportive model the therapist tries to underline the strengths of the patient and seeks to maximize the patient's autonomy. He can use suggestive techniques, actively try to structure the patients' life situation and offer comfort and reassurance. These techniques are not used in interpretative therapy.

9.  Transference: in the supportive model negative transference is addressed if it prevents progress in therapy, but positive transference is not discussed. In the interpretative model all aspects of transference are actively explored.

It is important to note that all kinds of therapeutic groups, as opposed to individual therapy, contain most of the supportive aspects. The therapist mainly has influence on the therapeutic focus (5), his own techniques (8) and the handling of the transference (9).

# Chapter 4

# Clinical examples

This section will offer several examples of how clinical groups may function, and includes vignettes, parts of sessions, one more complete session and a longitudinal description of selected aspects of the process. An important point of departure for understanding and intervening in the group will be the terms *configuration* and *localization*, so we will try to demonstrate several versions of this. The therapists' interventions will be guided by their understanding of configuration and localization, for example group-as-a-whole phenomena and sub-grouping, and we will try to organize the material according to these configurations. The interpretation will often include the configuration and localization, and although it may always directly or indirectly be addressed to the whole group, it may focus on what goes on in the group-as-a-whole, in sub-groups and with individual group members, including the therapist himself.

In addition to the dynamic matrix, the configuration will also be affected by the *stage* the group is in, i.e. opening, middle phase or closing. It is also important how mature or immature its working style is, the group *composition*, i.e. balancing male/female participation, withdrawing/externalizing members, variations in capacity for self-observation and psychological mindedness etc. Finally, it will be affected by whether the group is currently a *work* group or more or less characterized by resistance, e.g. by what Bion called dependency, fight-flight or pairing groups (1974).

Examples 1 and 2 are intended to demonstrate group-as-a-whole phenomena. Examples 3 and 4 clearly demonstrate a configuration characterized by sub-grouping. Example 4 is extensive, consisting of a more detailed description of one session, followed by excerpts from earlier situations in the group's life and that of several individuals. By focusing on single persons we want to demonstrate how individuals may be put in the foreground of the group, and also when the therapist may or may not use individual interpretations.

## Interpretation of the group-as-a-whole

### Example 1. Rivalry for attention and love

In the previous session, the therapist had told the group members that the group would get two new members in a few weeks' time. This session begins with a man saying that he has been to a wedding. He found it tiring meeting so many strangers, everyone was talking about their own thing and he felt small and overlooked. The bridegroom was an old friend of his and he had also felt a bit jealous of the best man, who had been talking and laughing with the bridegroom a lot. He had originally expected that he himself would be asked to be best man. A woman recalls that she had once been in a similar situation, when a teacher had asked a school friend of hers to recite a poem in a school show, even though she was much better at reciting poems. Another woman talked about her children, who were quarrelling a lot and who sometimes ended up fighting. The day before, they had got into an argument about how much pocket money they got, the youngest child claiming that he got too little. However, the quarrel could easily have been about anything, from who got the biggest helping of pudding to who got to sit in the front passenger seat next to their father when he was driving etc. A fourth member interjects, saying that a colleague of his at work has been sacked and that he feels happy about that, because this colleague is the sort of person who is always unhappy with things, the sort of person who is always finding fault and feels aggrieved because he thinks he has been treated unfairly. 'You have to find your own place in life and play the hand you are dealt without complaining.' A fifth member is surprised that there is so much fighting in the world. It seems to him that despite the fact that we have reached a stage of prosperity, where we are all actually doing quite well for ourselves, the number of people with nervous disorders just keeps increasing. The sixth member, who has just been sitting looking sad, asks if he can speak to the therapist after the session. Something terrible has happened in his family and he simply finds it too difficult to talk about this to the group, and he thinks he will only need a few minutes.

In this group we see a clear example of 'free group associations'. *The whole group* seems to speak and react in a particular way, as if it were a living unit. The individual members nonetheless express themselves in different ways and through different voices. All contributions are variations on the same theme, even if group members are not aware of the theme and are thus often uncertain about what they are actually talking about. The configuration is therefore characterized by 'free group associations', which is often the sign of a mature group.

The group process 'captures' each member, without them being aware of it. The associations are variations on the main theme of rivalry for love and attention, competing to be noticed and appreciated, often by an authority figure. This relates to the group member himself, his children or a colleague. One member sees no reason why things have to be like that, while the sixth member 'acts out' in the transference, by asking the therapist for extra time. 'The cause', i.e. the localization of all this, is the therapist's former announcement that he is going to admit two new members to the group, which activates events from the various members' lives. The degree of affective commitment, the extent to which they are directly or indirectly involved in what they are reporting and the size of the triggering incident may say something about how central this area of conflict is to the respective person. Their responses correspond to the developmental level that they are at.

Proposed interpretation: 'It seems as if everyone in the group is preoccupied with being noticed and recognized by an authority figure. We probably all know from experience what it is like to be overlooked, or to love someone without being loved in return. Many of you have probably also experienced how painful it is when others, such as siblings, are given what we have been longing for with all our hearts. Since this theme has become topical today, I think it might have something to do with my remark last session that I intended to admit two new people into the group. You seem to be thinking that there will be even more people with claims on the group's time and my attention.'

## Example 2. Loss of a therapist: the configuration evolves over several sessions

One group had to change therapist at short notice, at an early stage in therapy. In the first meeting with the new therapist, the members spoke freely, but the therapist himself felt totally ignored by the group. It was as though the group were in denial about the fact that they had a new leader. Eventually, they began talking about serious topics, such as suicide and terminal illness. When the therapist asked the group members why they were talking about such depressing things, he did not get an answer. Instead, the group went on to discuss how a woman ought to come to terms with the fact that her husband had left her. During subsequent meetings, other patterns appeared: member attendance started to change, a few group members had consulted their GPs about their problems and they told the group about this. Others came up with the idea of resolving their problems by getting a divorce and finding a new partner. Meanwhile, an elderly woman who had been strongly attached to the previous therapist had started to become scapegoated by the group, and the group talked about what kind of sanctions they should have against members who did not get so involved in the group.

The pattern here is that the seemingly contradictory communication, the acting out and transference onto the therapist, are 'configured' around the old and the new therapist. The cause of this is the loss of the old therapist to whom several members had become strongly attached.

Obviously, the new therapist should intervene and suggest to the group members some sort of 'understanding' of all this. Serious acting out, the possibility of changing therapists, divorce and scapegoating may be destructive for the group and the individual members if it goes on, all indicating that an intervention is desirable at this point. The interpretation (translation) could be made in a more tentative or challenging way, depending on how established or mature the group appears to be.

An example of a tentative interpretation: a start could be to describe the key affects of grief, anger or indifference. The therapist could also suggest that these feelings had been triggered by the sudden loss of the old therapist, to whom many group members had started to become attached. He may also suggest that this incident may have activated earlier episodes of loss. Depending on the response from the group members, the therapist may pursue individual stories that may be disclosed.

A more direct interpretation would be: 'It must have been frightening and disappointing for you that NN (the therapist), who was so important to you and the group, suddenly disappeared. You must also have been quite angry and maybe even experienced it as a betrayal. That may explain why, in many respects, I have been ignored, why the topics of divorce and people being abandoned by their husbands have appeared, and certainly why some of you have mentioned needing to talk to a doctor that you feel you can have confidence in.'

## Interpretation of sub-group phenomena

### Example 3. Sub-grouping: silence, medication, hostility and tropical fish

After attending a group for a few months, a young woman became strongly attached to the therapist, and at the same time she became hostile towards another female member, whom she did everything possible to ignore. In a particular encounter, the negative feelings of the young woman towards the other were in the foreground. At that moment, the background of the other group members' reactions was complex: two members were sitting in deep silence, two others were attempting to discuss a different topic, and one was addressing the therapist himself asking for a prescription for medication. Any of these phenomena might enter the foreground, thus displacing the interaction between the women, and might involve issues which were entirely different from what was being discussed. The communication in a given situation is configured around different 'dynamic centres' in the group. Based on his knowledge of the young woman and her family circumstances, the therapist assumed that the interaction she was involved in stems from pathological interpersonal relationships in her primary family. These have now become 'transferred' to the group situation and involve another group member. The two silent members are probably thinking of completely different things, and may currently feel too embarrassed to actually want to discuss what they are thinking of. The member who approached the therapist with a question about medication brought a prepared wish to the group that needed an immediate response. The last two members were more interested in discussing a programme on tropical fish they had seen on television the previous day.

In this situation it is impossible to grasp a common theme and the configuration is characterized by several sub-groups which are preoccupied with various activities or topics.

Proposed intervention: here, all the sub-groups should be explored further before anything more can be known about the background of the various constellations. Alternatively, one could choose a sub-group which seems particularly 'important', e.g. the largest or most emotional, and comment on it; one option is to concentrate on a single group member, another to simply comment to the effect that several fractions in the group seem to be preoccupied with their own topics and that they do not seem to be listening to each other.

In the next example, one session is presented in some detail. This offers an opportunity to describe and discuss the configuration of sub-grouping, as well as the topic of multiple transferences and some important therapist interventions, other than interpretations or translations. Multiple transferences and therapist interventions will be presented under separate headings.

Excerpts from this group will also be elaborated on later in the section on 'Interpretations on an individual level'. By giving detailed information of interactions and tracing individual reactions to particular events in the group's or individual members' histories, we will try to illustrate some of the richness of information embedded in the group matrix.

### Example 4. First session after summer break

The therapist opens the door to the waiting room, where a lively conversation is in progress, and says, 'Please, come in' and goes back into the treatment room. A woman in her forties enters first. She has a pretty face, but is somewhat overweight and her body is not very well toned. She sits down without meeting the therapist's eye. She is followed closely by a man of the same age, who scowls at the therapist. He says 'Hello,' and sits as far away from the therapist as possible. He is instantly followed by a slim, somewhat weasel-like man in his early fifties. He smiles, greets everyone and sits down. 'Hiya,' says a well-groomed woman in her thirties. She looks the therapist straight in the eye and gives him a broad smile. Her suit is fashionable and tight-fitting, she is wearing high-heeled shoes and a low neckline. The therapist answers with a curt, confused 'Morning,' and she sits down next to him. A third woman, in her late thirties, slim and sporty, wearing a scarf around her neck, creeps into the room, sits down at a distance and looks down. Finally, two men walk in, chatting, one in his thirties, pale, with a shaved head that would have been almost completely bald. He smiles broadly and says hello to everyone. The other is 50 years old and has a serious face, short hair, a beard, a moustache and is wearing glasses. Silence descends and the first group session after the summer break has started.

After a short pause, Else, the overweight woman who came in first, said tentatively, in a quiet voice: 'Perhaps I could go first today? I've been having such a difficult time lately. I don't think I've been getting any better at all.' She had joined the group a few months earlier, seeking help for an increasing depression and anxiety which had been triggered by problems at the school where she was teaching. Parents had made complaints about her teaching and the curriculum on several occasions. The children, however, were satisfied with her work and the head teacher stood up for her, but that did not really help. In addition, she felt that her life was slipping out of her hands. She had a good relationship with her husband and her teenage children, but they were all off doing things with which she could not join in, and she felt as if she was not needed any more. She continued talking about her worries, about all the responsibilities she had at school that were soon going to start up again: Yet another pilot scheme was going to be introduced and she was not sure if she would be up to the job.

Anders, the 50-year-old with the beard and glasses, started reassuring her that it would all go well. She seemed so competent and organized, so he was in no doubt that she would manage just fine. He is a health worker, married and has children. He sought help three years previously when his wife forced him to make a choice. She could no longer deal with his withdrawal from life, the fact that he would retreat to his bed at any opportunity and leave it to her to look after the house, garden and children. If he did not change, she would divorce him. He had also been absent from work a lot and soon slipped into the same withdrawal pattern in the group. However, he would occasionally give comments to the others in the group, often in a slightly superficial way.

After a brief, oppressive silence, the therapist began to ask questions about the details of the woman's conflict with the parents of children in her class. From her answer, it seemed that she actually had done a poor job, teaching a subject that she did not know much about. At the same time, however, it appeared that she had taken the parent's criticism of the new school scheme, which was not her responsibility at all, too personally. A couple of parents had also been quite tough on her. All this was beginning to come to the boil and she was blaming herself: 'I'm not good enough and I'm scared of failing again'. Several members had now got involved with her story and the picture had eventually become clearer.

The therapist remarked that it might be useful for her to work out whether her current situation has been caused by resignation and despair triggered by external demands, by her putting unrealistic demands on herself, by her lack of expertise or knowledge or by her poor treatment at the hands of others.

A brief silence ensued and then Rita, the woman who entered the room with a 'Hiya', starts speaking in a confident voice: 'I'm so proud of myself. I got my exam report back and I've been given top marks! I'm so incredibly happy that I coped with everything all on my own. Now I know that I'll be able to carry on with my studies for another year'. Several members chipped in with positive comments, but a couple, especially Hilde, the woman who had crept into the room with a scarf around her neck, stared pointedly in the opposite direction. Rita had sought help a couple of years earlier after reaching a dead end at work, where she had been feeling unhappy for some time. She had been afraid of resigning, not wanting to appear unhappy, because that might impact negatively on her references. She did eventually resign, however, and had started an educational course, not because she felt particularly interested in the subject, but because she 'wanted to be someone'. She was not married, she had had a string of short-term relationships, partly because she had a tendency to end up with men who were already married and partly because she had a tendency to get fed up with them before too long. At an early stage of the therapy, she could hardly bear any silence, and would involuntarily burst into giggles demanding that something happen, addressing the therapist in particular. Over time, she had become calmer and more reflective. She was now in a new relationship, which had been going on for a few months. She continued with the same theme by saying that they had a lovely time this summer and she had also met his children. It then transpired that she felt jealous, and that she got irritated by how badly the children were behaving, but she did not dare say anything, either to her boyfriend or to the children themselves. She had started feeling attached to him and was afraid of losing him.

Hilde was a health worker and had been in the group for six years. At this point she sighed loudly, seemingly irritated and physically restless. When this was pointed out to her, she replied that she did not wish any harm to anyone's relationship, but that she was 'not going to be able to bear listening to this love talk for much longer! There must be other things in life that matter!' This was a well-worn theme which everyone in the group had become familiar with. Hilde was in her early thirties when she sought help. Her life consisted of work, exercise and her cat. She had fixed opinions about herself and other people, like that her mother was 'a vicious psychopath who had ruined her life'. She felt that her problems were more serious than anyone else's in the group, and that the things that the others complained about were mere trifles. She had suffered from eating disorders in her teens, but had come out the other side, with the help of exercise, a healthy diet and self-determination. She felt incapable of managing a social life, not daring to open up to anyone and believing that others would reject her if they got to know her better. She despised smokers, people who were overweight or those who did not eat healthy food, those drinking alcohol, people who did not like animals or had casual sexual relationships. She had never had a boyfriend and her only friends had been little more than acquaintances. She had got into the habit of drawing the curtains and going to bed early and never went out except to exercise or go to work. She gave her undivided support to anyone she considered a victim of unfair treatment, even when the involved people themselves did not feel hurt. Eventually, she expanded her network by inviting colleagues home, disclosing some of her problems and the fact that she was in therapy. She got a positive response to this, but still often ended up being a 'mother' for others. She also had a relationship with a man that lasted a few months. When the relationship broke up, she was devastated and furious and fell into a moderate depression, from which she recovered with the help of medication. When she started feeling safer in the group, she would at times be overpowered by extreme rage, which scared both her and the others. Eventually, she would start making snide comments or aggressively challenge group members who talked about problems with their partners. She initially idealized the therapist, but her outbursts meant that the therapist often had to defend the other group members, which resulted in their relationship cooling somewhat and in her transferring aggression more onto him. Their rapport survived these knocks, however. The various split sides of her personality eventually became visible to the other group members, who accepted them as part of her and took more responsibility for giving her feedback.

Several group members contributed to the current session. Else was down and feeling insecure about whether she would be able to cope at work. Rita was excited about how clever she had been and her increased self-confidence was even more boosted by having been able to remain in a relationship for several months. Hilde aggressively complained that everyone's intimate relationships had once again been brought into the open. The session shows a configuration around these people. Three members remained silent, although following the session attentively and working quietly on their own. Several other members came into the foreground when making comments: one assured Else, fairly superficially, that she was going to cope well and a few members praised Rita for having passed her assessment.

All these issues can be localized in the preceding interruption of therapy as a result of the summer holidays. This break represented a 'failure' in relation to the group and the therapist and activated conflicts which centre on the question of attachment. Else and Rita were spokespersons for two different *sub-groups*: one was withdrawn and felt alone, Else was doing badly at work and felt betrayed, disappointed and angry and she blamed the therapist for this. Rita had been getting on brilliantly, coping completely on her own, without needing any help. We also heard that her attachment to her boyfriend had become stronger, but also that she was more anxious about losing him. Anders, whose wife issued him with an ultimatum, represented a thin defence, formulated as, 'We're going to be all right, it will probably all turn out fine'. Hilde had, a couple of months before the summer break, been told that her therapy would have to come to an end within the next six months. In this session she distanced herself by showing contempt for those in her immediate surroundings and her own longings for intimacy. She attacked and blamed Rita who had a boyfriend and, at the same time, denied her feelings for the therapist and, to a certain extent, the importance of group analysis, which is all about working with interpersonal relationships.

Proposed interpretation of sub-groups: 'It seems that there are three voices, in particular, that are arising in the group: firstly, the despondency and fear of failure or the fear that one is not going to be able to cope. Secondly, we witness a member taking pride in her success, in the fact that she has been coping on her own. Thirdly, we also hear about somebody's need to be with other people and the value of close relationships, but we also hear some severe doubts being voiced, whether having them in the first place is of any value. It strikes me as being no coincidence that these themes have arisen today, since the group has had to manage without each other and without me for so long during the break, and there have certainly been a lot of mixed feelings in this regard.'

## Multiple transferences

In addition to configurations and localizations, this example demonstrates *multiple transference reactions*: Else tells the therapist, without looking him in the face, that she is not doing well and that her situation has not improved. There is reproach in her words. Rita, who is sitting next to the therapist, is not open to any feedback other than praise for her academic results and believes that this success is down to her alone. However, her glamorous appearance, pleasant manners, the success she has talked about and her independence are slightly at odds with the uncertainty she exposes about her boyfriend and his children. The *transference* from the man with the glasses and the beard is characterized by the playing down and denial of conflict, while the third woman's aggressive outbursts bear a *projectional* hallmark, since she *devalues* the importance of relationships, thereby making the 'Hiya woman' the only carrier of the desire for attachment and belonging. The themes are the looming possibility of loss, coping and autonomy, in contrast to the ability to function in the workplace and in relationships.

## Therapist interventions

The therapist's question about the details of Else's conflict could be placed under the heading of *modelling*; he does something he wants the others in the group to do. His comments about what the cause of Else's resignation might be is an *open facilitating* intervention. He could have waited, but he thought that the pause had been long and unproductive, and he wanted to break the despondency by picking up on the details and nuances, in order to understand what lay beneath. Perhaps he was also struck by the criticism that she had not been receiving any help, which is a negative comment, alluding to the fact that she had been left to her own devices all summer. He possibly also had in mind Rita who claimed that she had been able to cope with everything herself, as if she had forgotten that, for a long time, the group had been involved, supporting her both in her struggles as a student and in establishing a relationship. A final intervention that had been presented in this group deals with confrontation and limit-setting in relationship to Hilde. A few months before the session in question, the therapist had told her that he doubted if she would further progress in therapy unless she was able to accept that the things she despised in others, also represented potential aspects of herself, which should be explored in the group. He also thought that it might be wise to think about ending the therapy, if this suggestion seemed meaningless to her. It was stated directly that in that way she would stop 'wasting her time', which were the exact words she had used herself earlier. Also the group would be allowed to work more constructively and move on. She half-heartedly agreed with this, but did not seem to take it properly on board. In response to the therapist's statement, the man sitting furthest away from the therapist launched into a diatribe about him 'being heartless'. Tempers flared and the group split into pro- and anti-therapist camps. This man had himself sought help a few weeks earlier because he had been feeling depressed and because he had been in a state of personal and professional stagnation, since his partner had left him two years previously.

Interpretations may also primarily be addressed to an individual group member.

## Interpretations on an individual level

When should one interpret on an individual level?

The prerequisite for interpreting on a group level is that the configuration, that is what the therapist is referring to, must be visible and that the 'localization' or the connection to a plausible 'cause' must be close to conscious life and can easily be demonstrated. Otherwise, the interpretation is more likely to be regarded as an attempt at facilitating intervention. Some studies (e.g. Malan *et al.*, 1976) suggest that interpretations at the group level may be perceived as impersonal and meaningless and that, if it is the only strategy used, this may produce a poor treatment result. There is, therefore, an empirical basis for the usefuless of therapists sometimes working with patients individually in the group as well. It may seem evident that the concepts of configuration and localization are more relevant in working with the group-as-a-whole and sub-group phenomena. However, the group may also be configured around single members. As one focuses on the role of single persons and dyads in the group, the concept of multiple transference(s) can make the picture richer and more complete. As a starting point, I will define a transference (reaction) in a broad sense. It may consist of as many as three components: First, the subject's wishes or fears towards another person, that may or may not be reasonable. Second, a distortion in the subject's expected responses from the person, and third, a reaction to these distorted responses. An example would be that a subject expects to be rejected and reacts as if this has happened, even though the other has responded in a warm accepting way. These contributions may be more or less characteristic for each person, as well as it may be so for the therapist's counter-transference. It is possible to restrict the interpretations to the framework which the here-and-now situation offers, but one can also draw on the there-and-then and past relationships. An interpretation at a group or sub-group level is often supplemented with one or more interpretations directed at an individual, or even the intrapsychic level. Interpretations should, however, be spread over time, as a group can easily be overwhelmed. It is also important to give consideration to providing an opportunity for the other members to make a contribution.

Here follow some reasons why one should interpret individually:

- When the group's development is being hampered by one or more individuals or their resistances, it may be necessary to work with individual patients. Early in the group, patients will display various degrees of ability to recognize psychological contexts. The pace at which they further develop this ability may also vary, which is why they may require various amounts of individual work in order to keep up with the group development.
- In order to demonstrate something which one has pointed out previously, but that the patient did not properly grasp. As a precondition, the individual concerned must have shown a genuine interest in finding out what was at the root of this.
- When an insight would benefit a particular patient given his problem area, and when this experience seems close to consciousness at the given moment.
- When someone is attacked in the group and if the therapist finds it necessary to protect the individual concerned.
- To hand projections back in the final phase of therapy.

When should one *not* interpret at an individual level?

- When the therapist is more concerned about 'winning a dispute', which will often be more related to acting out of counter-transference than to what the patient needs at the given moment.

- When the interpretation involves the therapist making connections which are not relevant to the patient's problems.
- When the group is doing a good job with 'free group association'.
- When more than one member has been involved in a critical situation and the interpretation might be construed as implying that a particular patient is being 'held responsible' for the event.
- When individual interpretations have proved fruitless in the past.

Here are some examples of when the therapist should *not* interpret at an individual level.

In Example 4, all the patients showed idiosyncratic reactions, rooted in the individuals' history. We see several transference reactions, onto the therapist, the other group members and the group-as-a-whole, for example:

1. In the changes in patients' facial expressions when greeting others and what they communicate by sitting down at a distance from the therapist.
2. In the exaggeratedly pleasant greeting combined with 'physical proximity' and an explicit appeal for praise.
3. In dissatisfaction and complaints that the treatment has not helped.
4. In the outrage over the therapist's 'heartlessness' with a patient who he wanted to terminate therapy.
5. In Hilde's projections onto Rita.
6. In the denial of Anders who thinks everything will be just fine.

Situations 1, 4 and 5: Two of the patients, Hans and Hilde, revealed a wish to distance themselves from the therapist. This impression is reinforced by their 'closed faces'. Hans was the person who had previously become furious with the therapist, while Hilde got angry with Rita. The therapist had tried to explore the incident described in the preceding section, but it seemed impossible to help Hans to reflect on how the confrontation of Hilde had affected him. His anger was not affected by the fact that the patient to whom the therapist had actually addressed his remark had not taken it to heart to the same extent. He was full of self-righteousness and any suggestion that his reaction also might have something to do with himself merely reinforced his rage. He was more interested in branding the therapist's 'heartlessness' than working with himself and he subsequently dropped out, devaluing the group and the therapist. The therapist also had tried to interpret Hilde's projections onto other group members, for example Rita. He worked with her tendency of projecting painful aspects of herself, her devaluation and black-and-white thinking directly in the group. Some improvement had been achieved, but the therapist decided that further improvement seemed futile. Besides, her attacks on other group members slowed down the group, even though the other group members were not as frightened of her anger any more. They were to some degree trying to get her to recognize and give up her own destructive patterns.

Situation 2: It would be wrong to interpret anything at an individual level for Rita, at least in this connection. While there may be some counter-phobic elements in her physical appearance, even if she perhaps denies having missed the group and the therapist over the summer holidays, and even though it would have been more appropriate for her to express gratitude for the help she received from the group's input, in addition to expressing pride in her own achievements, everything she communicated evidenced her progress. Moreover, she expressed a positive transference, which often translates as a positive impetus in group and individual development.

### Proposed interpretation at an individual level

Situation 3: Some aspects of Else's transference were touched upon above, when she was seen as a spokeswoman for one of the three sub-groups. The therapist suspected that her self-esteem largely depended on her being noticed, praised, appreciated and supported. When she did not feel recognized, she reacted with disappointment, discouragement, depression and self-reproach. This was the main reason why she had sought help, apart from problems at work and a sense that she was being taken for granted at home. The following interpretation from the therapist might be useful: 'You seem quite disappointed that you have not received more help in the group during the time you have been here. It seems that you are taking on the whole responsibility for this yourself. You are not alone here and some other person might perhaps have reacted with more anger or irritation towards me who failed to do enough (here-and-now). This reminds me a bit of what you have described at home, when the others do not take you along to any events or appreciate what you are doing for them' (there-and-then).

Situation 6: Anders exhibits a tendency to deny or play down problems, creating a kind of idyllic fantasy, with the aim of providing reassurance, mainly for himself that everything is fine. This is consistent with how he deals with many of the problems in his life and the kind of comments he often makes in the group. This was highlighted in the group when he tried to 'comfort' Else. The therapist did not comment on this, since his message could be seen as an *open facilitation*, asking Else to go on with her story.

The last example concerns a patient who almost always denied that anything that happened had a deeper meaning. In response to his attempts to generalize everything, like 'I guess we all go through such things, there is nothing really special about it', the therapist could comment: 'I get the sense that you seem quite anxious about there being a deeper and different meaning to some of the things that are happening, as if you constantly need to have everything under control. Based on what you told me about your childhood when your father kept a close watch on everything you did and said and frequently punished you, it strikes me that this has also started to apply to what you are thinking and feeling. It is as if you think you will be punished here, if you would tell us more about what is happening inside you.'

## Lack of configuration and localization

### Example 5. What is going on?

Most group therapists will often struggle to see a special configuration or localization. It is then important not to lose hope, since this is a part of each group therapist's life. Sharing this information with the group or colleagues may make it easier to resist the urge to *act in some unproductive way*, which may be a temptation for some.

Another solution could be to go on thinking about what the group's lack of configuration might mean; another to observe the group and look for interactions, while at the same time trying to observe one's own reactions. Could this be the actual transference onto the level of the group-as-a-whole? Has anything happened recently that has contributed to this regression and/or chaos? What kind of emotional colouring does the group have? A typical intervention would be to get the other group members involved in this questioning. Remember, group analysis is a treatment which is carried out in the group, by the group and of the group.

# Part II

# Short-term group analytic psychotherapy

# Chapter 5

# Theory

## Introduction

These guidelines have the same structure as the long-term guidelines and consist of four main sections: group theory, methodology, technique and clinical examples. Several aspects described for LTG will also be relevant for STG. Sometimes I may repeat some of the material that has been presented in the description of LTG. The purpose of this is to make it possible to start reading the guidelines for short-term group therapy directly, when STG is the primary interest. In order to avoid too many repetitions I will, a few times, when a section is identical, refer to the LTG guidelines, instead of repeating it here. Large parts of the theory and methodology sections of the STG guidelines are, however, different from the LTG guidelines, which entirely are built on group analytic theory. Under 'methodology' the main elements of short-term treatment will be presented: the group, the therapist's tasks, the treatment contract and the therapist's attitude and interventions, plus a model of the treatment and effective factors. In the section on technique I have included guidelines for interventions and given clinical examples showing *when* and *how* the therapist could use the interventions described in the section on methodology. I have tried to describe how the therapist in an empathic, consistent and flexible way may develop and work in the group.

Categorizations may also in these guidelines sometimes seem arbitrary because it may be difficult to place a topic within a specific section.

The short-term guidelines select ideas from many sources. Much of the material is built on my own clinical experience, including my own work experience and training in short-term therapy. Theoretically, Roy MacKenzie's book, *Time-Managed Group Psychotherapy*, has been a central inspiration and source (MacKenzie, 1997). He presents a generic short-term model, which I have transformed into a model for short-term analytic group psychotherapy.

## Defining short-term group analytic psychotherapy

Short-term group analytic psychotherapy, as described here, includes most elements that have demonstrated a positive relationship to outcome in empirical research (Orlinsky, Grawe, and Parks, 2004). The original model is not connected to any specific theoretical 'school', but I have emphasized and developed a psychodynamic perspective and rationale: a developmental perspective on personality, existence of internal representations of interpersonal relationships, psychological causation, influence of unconscious individual and group processes on behaviour, ubiquity of psychological conflict and the existence of psychic defences.

Short-term groups require modifications in some areas compared to long-term groups:

- greater therapist activity
- more structure
- more focused treatment problem
- more work in the here-and-now
- more attention to the termination phase.

## The objective of the therapy

This short-term form of therapy is an uncovering therapy that seeks to focus on the interplay and interactions between the members of the group in order to activate each member's intrapsychic conflicts and to correct irrational behaviours and interactional patterns that lead to or maintain personal problems and conflicts. Using new insights and having corrective emotional experiences leading to individual behavioural changes in- and outside the group may lead to a more realistic self-image, may stop dysfunctional patterns, and lead to the use of more adaptive, functional interpersonal strategies.

## View of human nature

Man is basically a social being, born into and reared in the family group. Families in concert with other families develop and constitute more complex social systems, i.e. society. Humans need to relate and communicate, and human behaviour may best be understood in a social context, which makes group psychotherapy an effective treatment medium. The cultural background that we share, i.e. having a body, being born into and socialized in a family, being dependent on each other, needing to communicate, use of language, etc., is of vital importance when it comes to understanding each other.

## Mental disorders

Even though the causes of mental disorders are complex and multidimensional, based in biology, inheritance, temperament, early external adverse influences, etc., most of them will be strongly associated with or influence human relationships. Disturbances may become manifest in the individual's relationship to the group, and will often have originated in the patient's closest relationships in the family, his primary group. Since mental disorders 'originated' in the relationships between the individual and his surroundings, group therapy makes it possible to demonstrate and analyze these disturbances, as a starting point for a deeper understanding and correction of dysfunctional human relationships. This also includes a change in experience of and attitude towards oneself.

## The therapeutic group and the therapy process

We can distinguish between (1) the patient's and the therapist's contributions or input to therapy, (2) elements in the therapy process itself, and (3) results or 'output' now and later, that is the impact of a single session, as well as changes taking place after termination.

### 1. What do the patients and the therapist bring to the group (input)?

For both parties there will be issues connected with socio-demographic status, like age, gender, family and social class, and everyone has a unique story concerning relationships, relational style and self-perception. Patients also bring their help-seeking position and often carry previous treatment experiences with them, which may colour their expectations. The therapist's role is defined by his or her professional role and status, theoretical orientation, professional experience and faculties as a person. Tensions because of differences in these areas, as well as other divergent opinions, will be activated early on in therapy. How they are handled will have an important impact on the further progress of the group.

### 2. The therapy process is complex and influenced by several factors

In individual therapy the therapeutic elements will be a product of the quality of the relationship between patient and therapist and the therapist's interventions. In a group the situation is more complex, since group members also will interact and engage with each other. The group atmosphere will be perceived as a product of everyone's contributions, which makes it necessary to consider the principles and dynamics of small group psychology. The following elements may be recognized (MacKenzie, 1997):

1. contract and preparation for the group
2. interaction and multidimensional feedback
3. group norms and treatment culture

4. group cohesion and other therapeutic factors
5. developmental phases in the group
6. therapeutic alliance
7. structure
8. the therapist's interventions
9. the significance of critical incidents (in-session impact)
10. the ability to use feedback and to have self-relatedness, which includes the capacity to reflect.

Most of these elements are relevant for several theoretical 'schools', even if they may have originated in just one of them. The concept of the therapeutic alliance, for example, comes from psychoanalytic theory and includes the working alliance, which implies cooperation between a 'realistic', more mature part of the patient and the therapist, in order to work on the patient's problems. Concern with structure and boundary incidents comes from systemic theory, the theory of group stages from studies of small group dynamics and the concept 'therapeutic factors' originated in interpersonal and existential psychology. Here, we want to apply a superordinate psychodynamic perspective on the group processes, interactions and the participants. We want to engage the patients in a psychodynamic treatment culture. The patients are prepared for this in the individual sessions before therapy starts, and the therapist models an analytic attitude in dealing with individuals, relationships in the group and the group-as-a-whole. Explicit norms, for example an instruction to be as open as possible, leaving aside too strict a self-censorship, may lead to interactions and transferences, which can be recognized and analyzed. The ability to use feedback (self-relatedness) refers to the patient's ability and willingness to observe him- or herself and to reflect about oneself in relationship to others. Disturbances in this area may materialize as individual resistance phenomena or lack of understanding. All these elements will be described in the sections on methodology or technique, but especially important approaches will be presented under separate headings:

• interaction and multidimensional feedback
• therapeutic alliance, group cohesion and other therapeutic factors
• developmental stages in the group
• the significance of structure and boundaries
• the therapist's interventions.

### 3. The effect of single sessions

The possibilities of change will vary during the course of therapy, and is a continuing process which hopefully may continue after the termination of therapy. Change can appear after a session and may have an impact on the person's view of himself and others, attitudes and general emotional state.

What the patient may learn in one session will be influenced by life events and the interaction with others between sessions, in addition to how important experiences are handled in later sessions. Any newfound 'wisdom' of the patient and attempts at changing behavioural patterns may be lost if life conditions are stagnant, or if people around the patient fail to give support or behave destructively towards the patient. If close relatives or friends are supportive, the positive effects may be increased.

Long-term results of therapy may largely depend on what and how much the patient has learned about themselves and others, how much of this has been worked through, and how intensely the patient has used this in order to change dysfunctional attitudes. An important aspect is also how much the patient has succeeded in developing more constructive interactions with his or her surroundings. Life events that we cannot influence are also important, for better or worse.

# Chapter 6

# Methodology

## General information about the group

I have given a more general description of the group structure, process and content in the Methodology section of LTG. That description is also valid for the STG manual (de Maré, 1972), and the main points are repeated here.

*The structure* of any group is defined by the physical arrangement, duration and frequency of sessions and of the therapy, the financial contract, as well as of any rules of behaviour in- and outside the group. The structure is also affected by the group composition and by whether the group is open or closed. *The process* of a group consists of communications and other interactions which develop in the course of a session, and from session to session – over time. *The content* deals with meaning, i.e. working towards a deeper understanding of statements and interactions. 'Deeper' means a pre-conscious or unconscious meaning in what is happening, in individual members, sub-groups and/or the group-as-a-whole. The therapist should assist in clarifying the latent content of statements and interactions, which in a short-term group especially should refer to the here-and-now, but also the group members' history and the social unconscious.

## Therapist responsibilities

The therapist's responsibilities are the same in STG as in the LTG: to engage everyone in the therapeutic process, to maintain the group's structure, to facilitate the group process and assist in understanding and giving interpretations. In STG interpretations should mainly refer to interactions in the here-and-now, and reference to historical events should be more sparse. An active use of specific group stages as a backdrop for interpretations (see 'Developmental stages in groups', pp. 49–52) are unique for STG.

## The contract between patient and therapist

The contract for STG will be similar to the one in LTG, except for a more circumscribed problem area as focus for the treatment and the duration. The main elements are an agreement to work in a group, basic rules regarding attendance, responsibilities in- and outside the group and financial arrangements. The therapist on his or her part will help patients understand and resolve the problems which have brought them into therapy.

## Interaction and multidimensional feedback

The group situation will, as opposed to individual therapy, offer a milieu for 'real relationships' with several persons, not only the therapist. More complex interactions, involving several persons at one time, are important in groups. Patients often experience more initial anxiety in groups when they present their problems, worrying about what the others think. A positive and accepting atmosphere will often result in an active self-disclosure early in the group, because patients 'copy' those who are more open. In short-term groups it is self-evident that everybody should be allotted some time, and this may be an impetus to start talking. The statement of group norms and a growing sense of cohesion may move things in the same direction. The process of trying to understand each other's problems will result in questions and comments from peer group members, as well as the therapist.

The responses early in therapy may be strongly subjective and coloured by the respondent's own problems. Feedback will, however, gradually become more 'objective', and patients also learn to reject feedback which seems too strange to them. The interactional milieu in the group makes it a more flexible learning situation than individual therapy. Patients who have been silent in individual therapy may open up because of the supportive pressure exerted by other group members. Some may give up their scepticism or parsimonious attitude when other group members disclose personal material.

The therapist will usually engage from the start in how patients relate to the multidimensional feedback they get, their lack of openness and interest in others, or their tendency to accept everything said and meet it with equal interest. The possible destructive polarization of 'power' that may be seen in individual therapy is often strongly diluted in the group, or readily becomes more visible when other group members comment empathically from the sidelines. In the group critical incidents involve more people, and the fact that different elements and persons continuously interact is the most complicated part of the model. However, one person may also become the focus of rejection or criticism from several group members or the whole group, which potentially may be destructive. The group is a potent medium!

Group processes often accelerate as a function of so-called therapeutic factors and may be coloured by developmental stages or norms that were established early in the group's life.

## Therapeutic alliance, group cohesion and other therapeutic factors

The therapeutic alliance is the strongest predictor of outcome in *individual* psychotherapy. It is also important in group psychotherapy although the process here is more complicated. Usually the patient's ratings of the alliance have a stronger relationship to outcome than therapist ratings or ratings from an independent observer. In group therapy, cohesion has traditionally been seen as the 'therapeutic alliance in groups'. Even though members may disagree about how cohesive a group is, a lot of research indicates that cohesive groups are more effective and have fewer drop-outs than less cohesive ones. Cohesion has been defined as the sum of all forces that keep members of a group together and consists of a feeling of belonging to the group, that single members feel accepted and that they are participating in something important.

A cohesive group may exert a considerable social pressure on individual members who try to 'hide' in the group. The therapist thus has many good helpers in working with resistances. Important incidents will usually involve several members, as opposed to the dyadic relationship of individual therapy. In this way group therapy has a larger 'in-session impact', or richer opportunities for corrective emotional experiences. This requires that patients and therapist are open and available for new learning (self-relatedness), and that interpersonal incidents are recognized, constructively handled and worked through.

Therapeutic factors constitute a separate research area in group psychotherapy (Yalom and Leszcz, 2005), and started when patients who had profited from group therapy were asked what they experienced as effective, important or helpful. Group cohesion is the most studied therapeutic factor and has a strong association with positive outcome. It is important to work actively to develop cohesion at an early stage in the group, especially in short-term groups. Group cohesion will, however, vary within and across sessions, influenced by for example negative or critical incidents. Good cohesion is probably a necessary precondition for making several of the following factors effective.

- Supportive factors:
  - o instillation of hope
  - o feeling of acceptance
  - o altruism (the wish to help others)
  - o universality (one recognizes oneself in others).

- Self-disclosure:
  - o to tell about personal things
  - o catharsis (to fully experience feelings).

- Learning factors:
  - o modelling
  - o vicarious learning (by imagining oneself into a situation)
  - o advice giving
  - o education (learning facts).

- Psychological elements, which require more active work:
  - o   interpersonal learning
  - o   insight.

These factors are considered to be so familiar for most people that I will not go into detail. All are important. The supportive factors are important early in therapy and may be a prerequisite for patients to be willing to be open about themselves, which again may lead to more interactions and further development of cohesion. The learning factors are important all through the therapy. From a psychodynamic point of view it is important that patients get to know more about their own intrapsychic conflicts and dysfunctional interpersonal patterns, and that this insight is used in trying out new ways of behaving inside and outside therapy. The interpersonal aspect gives a larger possibility for interpersonal learning. Both interpersonal learning and insight are closely related to the psychoanalytic concept of 'working through' and Foulkes' concept of ego-training in action.

## Developmental stages in groups

A well-organized group with a defined purpose and a competent leadership, that meets regularly over time, will develop through stages which, hopefully, will be productive for the goals of the group as well as individual members. These stages have been described somewhat differently by separate authors, but some convergent developmental lines exist. I have chosen a description of stages close to what MacKenzie (1997) has previously described for short-term groups: engagement, differentiation, interpersonal work and termination phase.

The climate in the group is usually increasingly coloured by the developmental phase of the group, and every stage offers a new interactional climate which allows the group to address new themes. During the engagement phase, supportive factors are often strongly mobilized. During the phase with interpersonal work, a more challenging attitude is to be expected, while attempts at reparation and the wish for group members to 'take their projections back' will manifest themselves in the termination phase.

The variance in experiences at different developmental stages of groups are especially salient for short-term groups. The group seems to concentrate on specific interactional tasks at each stage, which is reflected in typical forms of behaviour. Each stage seems to confront the group, individual members and the therapist with characteristic challenges that have to be solved in order for the group to be able to move on.

The rationale for using developmental phases in the therapeutic work is based on the experience derived from systemic thinking; that what takes place on one level will influence other levels. This means that the developmental process in each patient will resonate with the developmental process that

*Table 6.1* Overview of group stages, their duration and characteristics

| Stage | Duration | Characteristics |
|---|---|---|
| Opening, engagement | 2–4 sessions | Feeling of community 'What happens here is something special' |
| Differentiation | 2–4 sessions | Assert oneself and find strategies for handling of tension and conflicts |
| Interpersonal work | 8–12 sessions | Confrontation and introspection: work with own and others' dysfunctional interpersonal patterns |
| Termination | 2–3 sessions | Loss and separation: to have received enough in therapy and in life. Everyone is responsible for oneself |

takes place in the group-as-a-whole. Therefore it is important that all patients participate at each stage.

MacKenzie has offered a detailed overview of the developmental stages of the group (1997, p. 44) encompassing the tasks for individuals and the group, focus for boundaries, threats to individual members and possible attempts at solutions for individuals and group at each stage. A practitioner may easily find such a theoretical schema artificial and normative, containing mainly behavioural criteria, and fear that it may appear to be a 'straitjacket' that restricts the therapist. In reality, the group will often appear more differentiated, possibly with features from several stages occurring simultaneously. Thus I will present a more simplified version, which may possibly give more room for exploration of unconscious underlying forces in the patients and the group (see Table 6.1).

### Opening, engagement stage

The anxiety level may initially be rather high and the therapist should adopt a more active role in helping and instructing patients how to behave in order to manage and benefit from the group. Important tasks for the therapist in the two first sessions, in addition to making the room ready and greeting the patients, are to establish himself as leader, manage late-comings and promote a presentation of the goal for each patient's treatment. A central strategy in this phase is to develop cohesion by defining an external boundary, promoting interaction, clarifying group norms and use of therapeutic factors, especially the supportive ones. It is important to solicit reactions to what it is like to be in the group, since early detection of ambivalence and negative reactions may be of importance for preventing early drop-outs from the group. Group members will look for common themes and interests in this phase. They want to find similarities (universality) and often express feelings of 'being in the same boat'. Another central theme may be a growing recognition that the group is a unique place which has a set of rules on its own, different from conventional social rules. This strengthens the external boundaries of the group directed towards the outer world. The group's task at this stage is fulfilled when all members are determined to participate and when all to a limited degree have participated and disclosed some personal aspects.

### Differentiation stage

The atmosphere changes and becomes more negative and confronting. Disagreements or potential conflicts may emerge. An important task is to develop strategies for handling and solving tensions and conflicts that may appear. This means that group members must be taught a process of cooperation, where problems can be openly discussed. In contrast to the equality of the previous stage, patients now want to assert themselves as unique individuals, to state and show how they are different from others. Gradually the group members may present more problematic aspects of themselves, often problems connected to anger or shame. A consequence of a more confronting atmosphere may be that the members experience themselves as more different and complex than in the previous phase.

In this phase, the therapist is often challenged, possibly because the group members feel a need for expressing independence from the therapist's control. Some kind of 'youth revolt' may take place, seemingly often for the sake of the revolt, since many of the issues that are being contested are, in reality, open for negotiation in the group. When groups have problems in solving inter-member tensions, the group may often turn to the therapist expressing phantasies about who he is and what he means in a specific struggle. This stage may have a strong therapeutic potential for many, since the two central tasks of learning to address problems in a positive confronting way and to trust that the communication in the group will not be cut off, are central problems for many (neurotic) patients.

These two stages usually last four to eight weeks. If it happens that tension and conflicts do not emerge within the first six weeks, it is reasonable to assume that anxiety levels may be too high to negotiate this phase.

### Interpersonal work

The group is now capable of addressing the members' problems in a more direct and thorough way. The patients gradually take more responsibility for the group work and it is expected of them that they work with the problems that brought them to the group. The group, which now has the capacity to be both supportive and confronting, affords possibilities for exploring and confronting members and their interpersonal issues. The individual member may question themselves and be more introspective, while they at the same time may start exploring personal agendas with the group. The process, which includes the focus on individuality that started in the differentiation phase, is then consolidated.

The personal nature of the material will create a feeling of intimacy between members, and possibilities for exploring the relationships in the group will increase. This increasing sense of intimacy may sometimes also be romantically coloured, which again activates possibilities for rejection. Questions concerning self-esteem and trust become central themes when rejection is a possibility. While working with relationships, themes like independence, dependence, overinvolvement, autonomy, control, etc., are quickly activated, appearing in the here-and-now of the group.

### Termination stage

The group's last task is termination. This is an important, often painful task, especially in closed short-term groups when everyone ends at the same time. The group may often try to skip this phase, which reminds us of the therapist's responsibility to prevent this from happening. Several important themes come into focus in this phase:

- Patients may feel that they have not received enough, in a similar way they feel they have not gotten enough from their parents.
- They will have to work towards ending one or more relationships that have meant a lot to them.
- Previous experiences of loss will be activated.
- The patients are confronted with the fact that they are ultimately on their own.

All of these themes have strong existential undertones and are important in the maturational process. The emotional intensity in this phase is directly related to the time the group members have been together and how engaged they have become with each other.

This model of developmental stages in the group represents the background or context, that makes it possible for the therapist to orient himself in the process. At the same time it is a framework which gives meaning to interactions in the here-and-now situation.

## Therapist interventions

For STG, I basically recommend the same interventions as described earlier, under LTG. However, I have added two interventions that probably are used more frequently in STG, called 'staying with the focus' and 'switching to the here-and-now' (see clinical examples p. 56 and p. 66). Both are really composite interventions, borrowing elements from other interventions like maintenance of structure, facilitation as well as modelling. However, since they are especially important in STG, they are allotted a separate status here. Further specific directives for therapist activity in STG appear in the Technique chapter under 'Special issues in short-term analytic group psychotherapy' (see pp. 58–61).

In clinical practice it is usual to encourage patients to expose themselves verbally and through interaction with other group members, including the therapist. This will make it easier to achieve the objective of the therapy by creating the conditions whereby common and group-specific factors can become effective, in addition to more or less patient-specific interventions from other group members, including the therapist.

The following is an overview of the therapist's interventions in STG (the first eight are also described under LTG, see pp. 17–22).

### Maintenance of structure

This is an action whose aim is to clarify or confirm a limit, which may include the place, time, membership, task or rules. This can apply to the whole group or an individual member, including the therapist.

### Open facilitation (of process)

An intervention which simply aims to move the group forward. It is not based on any particular interpretation or hypothesis by the therapist, nor does it relate to any unconscious level of understanding.

### Guided facilitation (of process)

This intervention is used when the therapist has a hypothesis or interpretation in mind and gives the group a 'steer' towards it, e.g. through a question or observation, in the hope and expectation that they can do the rest of the work themselves.

### Interpretation (of contents and form)

Interpretation consists of a verbal intervention from the therapist which puts words to feelings or to meaning that is latent in the group-as-a-whole or in what individual members say or do.

In group analysis, where the therapy process consists of an ever-increasing expansion and deepening of communication, the term 'translation' is often used instead of 'interpretation'. What I understand by this term is a more tentative approach. One works from 'the surface', keeping open other possibilities for the understanding of phenomena, whilst avoiding unilaterally asserting oneself as an authoritative specialist on the unconscious mental life of others, which could adversely interfere with the development of a group analytic culture. However, situations may arise where it is important to take responsibility and to be clear when one feels sure about a particular situation. Autonomy and natural self-assertion is also part of the group-analytic culture.

### No immediate response

This reflects the fact that much of the therapist's behaviour consists of silent observation. Depending on the situation in the group, the therapist will sometimes refrain from saying or doing anything in order to see what happens, whilst reserving the right to intervene at a later stage depending on the group's further development.

### Action

Action covers any physical activity which the therapist has to undertake in the group, for example, for different reasons leaving his chair or touching another group member.

### Self-disclosure

Self-disclosure is any statement by the therapist about the content of his internal world (thoughts or feelings) or external world (facts) which does not fit into any of the other categories.

### Modelling

Modelling consists of all behaviours which the therapist carries out with the implicit intention that they be adopted and become part of the group's or members' repertoire. This includes, for example, mastering stressful events or unpleasant social situations or modelling an analytic enquiring and compassionate attitude.

### Staying with the focus

This point involves all therapist actions that intend to bring the patient back to the focus for his treatment (if he is astray) or to transform a more global, impressionistic, unspecific interest in a topic to a personally relevant, emotionally charged private issue (see p. 66).

### Switching to the here-and-now

This involves turning the group members' attention and interest from narratives of past or present events being reported, to actual or potential here-and-now interactions in the group (see p. 66).

## Therapist attitude

The importance of the therapists' attitude, how they behave, who they are and what they say and do, has been described in several points in the chapter on technique under LTG. Also in STG it is important for the therapist to know something about what impact he or she has on others, and because of the importance the therapist's attitude has in group analytic therapy, many of them are repeated here.

1. Maintain an expectation that patients should speak and get involved in what others are saying or doing. Patients then become active participants, not passive recipients of the treatment, and they will be continually confronted with situations which they have to tackle actively, which is itself an exercise in interpersonal relationships.

2. Patients should be encouraged to put aside self-criticism, by being told that they are expected to communicate what they are thinking as and when different ideas crop up. It may be helpful to emphasize that a therapy group is different from an ordinary social situation in this particular respect.

3. Patients should also be encouraged to explore aspects of themselves and the group, including unpleasant feelings. By accepting and encouraging statements which would not normally be tolerated in an ordinary social situation, the therapist is a model and demonstrates that direct communication of personal feelings and experiences is desirable.

4. The group gives a good opportunity to actively demonstrate that interactions are situations where subjective worlds meet, where everyone may have something to learn. A statement which one member addresses to another at an early stage in the process will often have a strongly projectional stamp. All statements are important, nonetheless, and the therapist should show interest in the patients' subjective impression of the therapist and of other group members.

5. Links should be charted between the patient's relationships with other people in his life outside therapy and his relationship with the therapist and other group members.

6. In short-term therapy it is more urgent that the therapist keep the focus on patients in the here-and-now situation, more than on relationships involving the patients and significant others outside the treatment situation, in the there-and-then. Because less time is available, narratives that patients bring to the group about other people in the present or the past have to be limited, and the material which is activated in the group through interaction between members should have priority. This does not apply unconditionally, for example if patients associate their other present or past relationships with what happens in the group. This, in fact, creates the basis for emotional learning and understanding. Nor does

it apply when patients bring to the group emotionally loaded fresh events which are greatly preoccupying them. Such events often provide good learning opportunities for them and for others, while emotionality 'awakens' the group.

Long intellectualizations about why things are the way they are, or repeatedly bringing up an ongoing relationship from outside the group when the atmosphere in the group becomes uncomfortable, should be addressed: 'It seems to me that you have told this story many times before without it having apparently helped you to move on. I think it would be very interesting if you could tell me when you experience something similar here, so we can look into it'. Or, in the latter case: 'Did you notice that, when it was getting a bit tense between you and NN, you started talking about . . .?'

In conclusion to this section I would like to emphasize the importance of four methodological issues that are especially important in short-term psychodynamic group therapy: The first point is (a) the importance of developing a group-analytic culture built on the principles that were developed under methodology, including to think about context or 'stages'. Next are the principles of (b) staying close to the focus and (c) to mainly work in the here-and-now and to switch if the group repeatedly lands on story-telling. The last point is (d) to be constantly aware of the impending termination of the group, and be sure to remind the group about this.

# Chapter 7

# Technique

## Preparation of patients
(see also p. 13 under LTG)

In addition to being an opportunity for the therapist to evaluate the patient and his problems, the pre-group individual sessions represent a situation where patients can be informed about what to expect from the treatment and what, on the other side, is expected from them. They should discuss possible goals for the therapy and some of the issues (tasks) they have to deal with in order to reach these goals. These sessions are important in building an initial alliance between the therapist and the patient, which will make it easier for the patient to enter the group. Further, this initial work paves the way for the development of a group culture that, hopefully, will be supportive and productive in the future work of patients and therapist, alike.

## Guidelines for interventions

The therapist's main activities are the same in STG as in LTG and mainly consist of observation, reflection and intervention, which partly take place in succession but also partly overlap each other. Instead of repeating a further elaboration of these aspects here, I will refer to the guidelines for LTG (pp. 14–22).

The most important is that all reflections and planning of interventions should be done in the light of group developmental stages, which is the backdrop and an important part of the context in which the members' and the group's behaviour should be understood.

The therapist's time is spent listening, observing and thinking (reflecting), and this activity precedes all interventions, including interpretations. The reflecting role is important and a necessary prerequisite for any of the outlined interventions one chooses. The therapist uses his observations, his perceptions of the individuals or the group, including knowledge of the patient's or the group's history. Emotionality, distribution of affects, the words used, topics, similarities and differences, the way things are expressed, are all important aspects in this work. In addition, the therapist considers contextual factors too: is anyone missing? Do we have any new members? Has the therapist or anyone else been ill? Did anything happen in the last session which may have caused a strong reaction in someone?

The important overriding principle of leaving the work to the group to resolve as many issues as possible is important in STG as in LTG. The therapist should hold back, if the group works well. However, in STG there is less time, and the therapist has to be more alert to the fact that he or she has the main responsibility for creating and maintaining a therapeutic culture that provides the optimal conditions for reaching the objectives of the therapy. Ideally, the group's role is to capture the meaning and to place that which is happening in an appropriate dynamic setting. However, the therapist should intervene when the group becomes unproductive.

## Special issues in short-term group analytic psychotherapy

The short-term perspective is central for the therapist's attitude to the group. There is less time available for each patient to express himself, to relate to the therapist and others, for working with the resistance, for working through and for making the unconscious conscious. This leads to technical modifications in running STG as compared to LTG.

### Increased therapist activity

The short-term therapist needs to be quicker in his thinking and should combine the capacity for introspection and reflection with the capacity to be energetic in the widest sense of the word. 'Energetic' here does not mean to be officious, acting or domineering, but to make correct strategic choices and do what is necessary to promote the process in relation to the overall goals of the treatment and within existing boundaries.

### More structure

From what is said above, the short-term therapist will be to some degree more structuring than a long-term therapist. He will make greater use of boundary events to make clear and highlight the idiosyncrasies of the patients and to promote the progression of the group through the different developmental phases (see p. 60).

### Focusing on problems

The therapist must decide how much historic material from the patients' past or from their current lives outside the group should be taken up in the sessions. He must also decide to what extent the patients should work with problem areas, which seem to be peripheral to what they wanted help for. He also has to prioritize between individuals and to make up his mind as to what is the most important aspect at the moment: to work with the group-as-a-whole or with individuals. Should one discuss a theme more broadly or focus on the lack of emotional engagement in the discussion? In short-term therapy one would generally prefer the last option.

### Focusing on the here-and-now

Even though the narratives the patients bring to the group may be emotionally loaded and thereby effective in activating central themes in other group members, the amount of 'storytelling' should be limited in a short-term group. The main focus must be the patients' problems as they manifest themselves relationally in the group (i.e. in relation to the therapist and other group members). This does not mean that patients in crisis cannot work with their most pressing external problems and certainly the group may from time to time need a push, if emotionality goes low, to allow the current relations in the group to be brought back into focus.

### More attention to the ending

The time the group and its members have at their disposal will tend to structure the developmental process of the individuals in the group. This structuring is determined by more or less conscious forces in the patients, such as ego-strength, type of defence, degree of traumatization, type or degree of psychopathology, etc. Patients may vary greatly. At one extreme you have the patient who consciously wishes to go into therapy, but quickly regresses and needs another sort of treatment than what short-term therapy can offer. Hopefully, a good evaluation and selection will make this an exception. However, it may be necessary to remove the patient from the group or see that he gets medication and sometimes even individual therapy. At the other extreme, you have the patient who never 'starts' therapy and passes 'untouched' through the process, which mainly takes on the characteristics of an intellectual exercise. Most patients, however, are going to engage in the therapy process, but may to a greater or lesser extent resist the ending as it approaches. It will be helpful if the therapist, from the start, tries to picture how the ending could be for each patient and how that might influence how to work with individual defences and what could be activated in the group for this patient. This often involves an understanding of the patient's specific way of handling separation, which can be the object of analysis in the last stage.

Moreover, the therapist must more than in long-term therapy take into consideration how his interventions are perceived by the group. The reduced time in STG will sometimes prevent the therapist from exploring the different reactions in the group fuller. This may also affect the therapist's capacity for reparation of the effects of earlier damage. It may be more difficult to focus on individuals and interventions may more often focus on the group, in an attempt to influence group climate or group cohesion. The strength of the therapeutic alliance and degree of cohesion in the group guide the therapist's interventions. Individual crises may make it necessary to pay extra attention to one patient. It is important to leave as many interventions as possible to group members. They will continuously put forward ideas, suggestions and personal experiences, that may function as comments to, or interpretations of, earlier contributions from other group members. All this is 'food for thought' and these spontaneous reports are often better received than the therapist's filtered, clinical comments. Interpersonal confrontations happen early in the group, which is a challenge to a member's accepted and often cherished inflexible opinions and viewpoints. Groups are also capable of mobilizing strong support through identification and empathic understanding. The way a member takes on a role in the group is decisive for the kind of interventions he receives.

## The importance of structure and boundaries

The structure is determined by group size, time and space, rules, physical location, paying arrangements, etc. All these structural elements have psychological correlates and implications. Strict rules can contribute to rigid norms; bad accommodation can lead to lack of concentration; negligence of time to chaos; an open door creates insecurity and represents a poor boundary between the group and the world outside, etc.. The concept of boundaries is central to group psychotherapy and the group's boundaries are the psychological dimensions of its space. One way to recognize a boundary is to have a clear feeling of differences, depending on being on one or the other side of the boundary.

The structural elements outlined above colour a member's group participation and makes it into an experience that is totally different from any other social situation. When members early in the life of the group start to talk about themselves, they will quickly experience that talking about oneself in this group is something different from what they experience when they talk about themselves in other circumstances, for example a party The acknowledgement of the differences of the interpersonal climate inside and outside the group consolidates the experience and psychological location of the group boundary. In the same way, we may talk about the boundary between the individual and the therapist, interpersonal boundaries between group members and boundaries around a sub-group.

The demonstration of and comments upon specific boundaries in the group is the first step in an important therapeutic strategy. How a person treats and perceives boundaries may be instructive to all persons involved in the group. By focusing and commenting on these events, continued consistently over time as specific behavioural patterns may repeat themselves, the therapist as well as other group members may promote a useful dialogue about what happens in the boundary areas, which may lead to insight and new interpersonal learning.

How to understand boundary incidents may depend on the stage the group is in. Here are some examples:

Two members who are frequently looking at each other across the room could at an early stage be understood as expressing mutual identification. This can be used in different ways by the therapist to promote group cohesion. In the engagement phase he can by means of a single comment suggest that they seem to experience a certain fellowship as they are occupied by some of the same questions. They will quickly get supported by others who will then constitute a sub-group, which will attract the attention of some more members. At this stage the therapist wants to develop a feeling of universality, 'we are all in the same boat'. This will strengthen the outer group boundary. In later sessions during the phase of differentiation or interpersonal work, the same observation could lead to exploring a sub-group process that hinders development or openness in the group. In the ending phase the same behaviour could represent grief in relation to separation and being busy with saying goodbye and reparation of earlier hurts etc.

Many of the patients' idiosyncratic ways and personality traits become clearer through boundary events. How do members relate to the group as a whole? Are they often late, are they blurting into the room interrupting what is going on, or do they stay away instead of coming late? How do patients relate to the boundaries of other members, including the therapist? Does a member continue to talk after it is announced that time is out? Did the patients talk about relevant group material in the waiting room, but become silent when entering? Is the therapist a reified machine that has to be endured? Are fellow patients consistently treated as advisers or an audience or are the inner boundaries so strong that silence and poker faces dominate?

The preoccupation with boundaries relates to the system theoretical approach that has been adopted in short-term and long-term psychodynamic group psychotherapy alike. The short-term perspective demands that the therapist is more active in relation to boundary incidents, than what is necessary in a longer term perspective.

## The dimension of support – activation/challenge

These are very similar in STG and LTG, but will be repeated for the ease of reading.

It is both impossible and futile to try to prescribe how the therapist should behave in all situations! The idea behind this section is that the therapist's approach may be more or less anxiety provoking. Also, his attitude and interventions may be graded according to a scale from 'very supportive' to very 'activating'. 'Very activating' has been equated by MacKenzie (1997) with 'very interpretative', but here it is used in a wider sense (see below).

The therapist has always to adapt himself to the patients' and group's needs. These needs depend on the category of patients being treated, the stage of the development of the group, as well as variations in anxiety level, generated within a single session. Degree of cohesiveness and therapeutic alliance are important hallmarks. An important question which constantly appears for the therapist is: what mixture of support and activating strategies is most useful in a given situation?

The therapist's interventions should ideally lead to increase in cooperation and positive alliance, and a strengthened cohesion in the group. Short-term groups do not give opportunity for extensive repairs of the therapeutic alliance, which may make this dimension slightly more important in STG than in LTG.

Some research indicates that supportive techniques are also important factors in the treatment of better integrated patients. In order to differentiate between more supportive and a more activating interpretative therapy, I will include some slightly reworked points from MacKenzie (1997).

1.  The therapeutic alliance is important in both supportive and more interpretative therapies.
2.  Technical neutrality: in the supportive model the therapist is more transparent, and feels free to express acceptance, respect and liking for the patient. In the interpretative model the therapist will only deviate from technical neutrality as much as is needed to preserve the therapeutic alliance.
3.  Therapist attitude and style: in the supportive model the therapist is more conversational. The therapist should be professional, but is to a larger degree focused on 'the real relationship' than in the interpretative model. Longer silences and lack of answers to the patients' questions are banned. In the interpretative model the therapist to a larger degree maintains a reticent position.
4.  Goal-directedness: in the supportive model the conversation is goal-directed, while the therapist in the interpretative model encourages free-floating associations and discourages pre-planned themes.
5.  Therapeutic focus: in the supportive model the therapist seeks to identify and describe patterns on a behavioural, cognitive or interpersonal level in order to modify them. Underlining of progress (improvement), instillation of hope and praise may be used. In the interpretative model the therapist emphasizes more affective aspects and interpretations that seek to connect intrapsychic conflicts between wishes and motives with present anxiety. In the interpretative model the self-esteem is expected to improve as a consequence of better functioning and insight.
6.  Handling anxiety: in the supportive model one tries to avoid therapy-related anxiety and picks it up immediately if it appears as a side effect of

the work in the group. In the interpretative model it is expected that therapy-related anxiety may increase as a consequence of the therapist's more expectant attitude. It is only addressed directly if it becomes destructive.

7.   Handling defence: in the supportive model the defences are to a larger degree left alone, unless they are extremely immature or destructive. In the interpretative model it is a goal to understand defences, and why they are needed.

8.   Therapist techniques: focusing, reframing, clarifications and confrontations, as well as challenging, are used in both models. In the supportive model the therapist tries to underline the strengths of the patient and seeks to maximize the patient's autonomy. He or she can use suggestive techniques, propose changes in the patients' life situation and give comfort and reassurance. These techniques are not so widely used in interpretative therapy.

9.   Transference: in the supportive model negative transference is addressed if it prevents progress in therapy, but positive transference is not questioned to the same degree. In the interpretative model all aspects of transference are actively explored. It is important to note that all kind of therapeutic groups, as opposed to individual therapy, contain most of the supportive aspects. The therapist mainly has influence on the therapeutic focus, his own techniques, and the handling of the transference.

# Chapter 8

# Clinical examples

## Examples of different types of interventions

Concerning the ten different therapist interventions described under 'Methodology', there are few or no differences in LTG and STG when it comes to 'open facilitation', 'no immediate response', 'action' or 'self-disclosure' (see pp. 19–21). This means that the clinical examples from LTG also should be relevant for STG. In addition we have included two interventions that are especially important in STG, 'Staying with the focus' and 'Switching to the here-and-now' (see pp. 54, 58, 59 and 66). 'Maintenance of structure' is also very similar in both formats. However, as mentioned earlier, in STG boundary incidents should be monitored and used more actively (see p. 60). This may more quickly give the therapist an understanding of individual problems as well as disturbances in the process, and provide the information that may be used to promote the group process further (see examples in the previous section).

### Guided facilitation

This intervention addresses aspects in the process and indicates that the thera-pist has a 'hypothesis' that in some way resonates with central psychodynamic themes on an individual or group level or in regard to the group's develop-mental level. The example above where the therapist states that exchange of gazes is an expression of a wish for finding others 'in the same boat' may be seen as a guided facilitation because it brings focus onto a central theme within the opening/engagement phase.

Examples of facilitating interventions in differentiation, work and termi-nation phases: members of a group take turns in blaming themselves because they fail in being open, that they are unable to make use of things they learn in the group in daily life, etc. A guided facilitating intervention in the differentiation phase might sound: 'I wonder if this discontent expressed by people, and the self-blaming, really expresses disappointment with me that I have failed to demonstrate how the group may be useful for you.' The under-lying hypothesis is that patients hesitate to assert themselves and to challenge the therapist, something that may be quite common in this phase. Or: 'In the first sessions we talked a lot about being in the same boat, that people seemed to have the same problems, etc. I wonder if by taking all the blame yourself, you turn your backs on something that is really a common task. What I mean is that in community we might find ways of exploring similarities and differences, even though this will mean that we are not always in agreement with each other'.

In the working phase a guided facilitation might sound like: 'I wonder if this is a reaction you are familiar with from other challenging interpersonal situations? We now have the opportunity to get to know both ourselves and others, but some or most of you seem to sit resigned on your own island.' This might be sufficient, or the therapist could add: 'What do you think is the reason why more people do not directly relate to others in the group?' The hypothesis is again that group members hesitate to address the group-specific tasks of this phase including confrontation, introspection and working with one's own and others' dysfunctional interpersonal patterns. Another possibility would be to interpret the group-as-a-whole: 'The group seems to be very sad, sort of depressed. I can hear self-blaming, which means that blaming others may be right around the corner. Some of you do have problems with expressing aggression, some have told me they rather work double shift instead of asserting themselves. I think this is what we are experiencing here now.' The therapist is sharing his hypothesis with the group.

In the termination phase a guided facilitation might be: 'We do not have much time left for the therapy, and I wonder if this sense of resignation hides an ocean of different feelings connected to this?'

### Modelling

Everything the therapist says in a group may easily get special significance. Through his attitude, way of being and by intervening, the therapist models behaviour he wants others in the group to adopt. Firstly, he wants to develop a treatment culture suitable for short-term therapy, that the patients can be a part of. Next he wants the patients to 'internalize' the therapist and the therapeutic function in order to continue the treatment on their own, after the termination of therapy. This includes for example the therapist's and the group's supportive and benign controlling function, which may be useful for neurotics with their strict superego, as well as some patients with personality disorders, who often have a defective, rudimentary superego. Everything the therapist does to demonstrate how he thinks, reflects and comments in a psychodynamic group becomes an example of potential modelling behaviour.

Examples:

- 'It is good that you express your irritation; that you show that you are engaged in what is happening here.'

- 'I wonder what is behind the bickering we have in the group now?'
- 'Boredom or being bored is some kind of grey shadow that sometimes covers up stronger, underlying feelings.'

### Staying with the focus and switching to the here-and-now

These are both composite interventions that remind us of the complexity of the therapist's tasks and the necessity of evaluating the situation, to intervene and consider potential consequences of the intervention 'simultaneously', or at least in quick succession. The therapist should, ideally, have a certain talent for multi-tasking.

Examples:

- When a patient gives a long, dry and detailed description of a movie he saw on TV the previous night, he may still be talking about something close to the focus of his therapy. The therapist should limit the story-telling (structure) and appreciate his contribution (confirm). At the same time a connection must be established between the sadness the patient felt and the tears he shed when the heroine was saved out of the burning house (in the movie) and events from his private life: for example that he often felt let down, when mother was unable to protect him from his father's temper tantrums and physical abuse in childhood. This may require use of open and/or guided facilitation, more structuring, possibly interpretations. At the same time the therapist models an attitude of exploration and enquiry.
- A similar chain of interventions may be necessary when the therapist wants the patient and group to chart a link between past or present events outside the group to the here-and-now interaction. The therapist can appreciate the story told, and then ask: how do you think these events have marked you, and how will that affect the way you may appear in the group? Or: these experiences have really been fundamental in your life, and I think it is very important that you tell us when similar feelings (feelings of being let down, sadness, despair, etc.) appear here, so we may work more closely with your problems.

### Interpretations

This intervention has traditionally been regarded as the most important intervention in psychoanalysis. Interpretations should, contrary to facilitating or modelling interventions, be presented in an articulate language. It is important that the patient understands that this may be one of many possible formulations, that this is a formulation of *this* therapist, and that it may be coloured by the therapist's counter-transference and personality. This should be communicated implicitly, or explicitly, if necessary. The interpretation may be addressed to one individual, to the interaction between individuals, to sub-groups or the group-as-a-whole. Examples of these interpretations follow below. Some of the ideas that were presented in the long-term therapy sections will also appear here.

## Individual interpretations

When should one interpret at an individual level?

The main issue in STG is that interpretations to a larger extent should refer to interactions in the here-and-now than in LTG, and they should be related to developmental stages in the group.

As mentioned under LTG, some studies (e.g. Malan *et al.*, 1976) suggest that interpretations at the group level may be perceived as impersonal and meaningless and that, if it is the only strategy used, may produce a poor treatment result. There is, therefore, an empirical basis for therapists being required to work with patients individually as well. Multiple transferences offer a rich material for interpretations, and may include individual impulses and defences, interpersonal events as well as sub-group and group-as-a-whole phenomena. Individual interpretations may be intrapsychically focused, for example, addressing how the patient is keeping facts hidden from himself, or a relationship may be in focus, i.e. how and why each group member is 'colouring' this in their own characteristic fashion. Here, one can also include any fellow patients with whom the individual in question has been colluding, or his relationship with the therapist. An interpretation at a group or sub-group level can also be supplemented with one or more interpretations at an individual level. These should, however, be spread over time, as a group can easily be overwhelmed. It is, of course, also important to give consideration to providing an opportunity for the other members to make a contribution.

I can think of the following reasons why one should interpret individually:

- When the group's development is being hampered by one or more individuals or their resistances, it may be necessary to work with individual patients. Initially, patients will display various degrees of ability to recognize psychological contexts. The pace at which they further develop this ability may also vary, which is why they may require various amounts of individual work in order to keep up with the group development.
- In order to demonstrate something which one has pointed out previously, but that the patient did not properly grasp. As a precondition, the individual concerned must have shown a genuine interest in finding out what was at the root of this.
- When an insight would benefit a particular patient given his problem area when this experience seems close to consciousness at the given moment.

- When someone is attacked in the group and if the therapist finds it necessary to protect the individual concerned.
- To hand projections back in the final phase of therapy.

When should one *not* interpret at an individual level?

- When the therapist is more concerned about 'winning a dispute' (acting out of counter-transference?) than about what the patient needs at the given moment.
- When the interpretation involves the therapist making connections which are not relevant to the patient's problems.
- When the group is doing a good job with 'free group association'.
- When more than one member has been involved in a critical situation and the interpretation might be construed as implying that a particular patient is being 'held responsible' for the event.
- When individual interpretations have proved fruitless in the past.

## Combinations of group-as-a-whole, sub-group and individual interpretations

As noted above, an absolute prerequisite for all interpretations is that the phenomena the therapist refers to should be 'visible', that the connections are close to give meaningful emotional resonance and can be demonstrated. If these conditions are not present, the interpretation may more be seen as an attempt of a facilitating intervention. Especially in short-term groups, the difference between guided facilitation and interpretation on sub-group or group-as-a-whole level may not be obvious and they may not be mutually exclusive categories. One requirement for calling an intervention an interpretation is that the therapist links the group's or sub-group's behaviour or interactional pattern and affective state together with the phase-specific challenges or themes, i.e. the actual developmental stage of the group.

Interpretations should be reserved for groups that have some degree of cohesion and which are in a differentiation, working or termination stage.

Notwithstanding the concerns noted above from Malan *et al.* (1976), what follow here are suggestions for how to interpret on the sub-group and group-as-a-whole level, possibly combined with interpretations on an individual level in STG at different stages.

### Example 1. An empty chair

The session starts and two of the chairs are empty. The patients may appear late for the session, but it is also possible that they will be absent for the whole session. The therapist may have been informed of apologies, but may also be as ignorant as the other group members. Maybe they are hosting phantasies that these missing patients may be potential drop-outs. The therapist waits in order to observe the group's reaction, and only later in the session will he or she comment on the reactions in the group, or the lack thereof. The therapist's intervention may be to explore themes that are related to feeling abandoned, angry, disappointed, betrayed, guilty or relieved that a certain person is absent, and to elicit the group's reaction to the absence. The response may also be identification with those absent and envy, imagining them spending their time somewhere else, having fun. This can be seen as a projection of people's own ambivalence about being in the group onto those who are absent. Closer to the end of the session the therapist may introduce an interpretation, trying to tie the different reactions of the members to an issue that is specific for the phase the group is in.

In the differentiating phase: 'The group seems to host rather mixed feelings concerning the empty chairs. Some members are angry and feel let down by Ole and Bente who chose to be somewhere else today, while some may feel responsible for having scared them off. We do not really know what has happened, but we can also detect envy in some because they think the absentees are enjoying themselves somewhere outside the group. I think we react according to who we are and our background. Another factor may be that we have started to show more of ourselves, and that we try to find acceptable ways of cooperating, which makes the group especially vulnerable to absences.'

In the working phase: 'I think that we react according to who we are and our background, but in order to understand the reactions here, it is important to look to what is happening in the group these days: There have been some confrontations, Ole disclosed many things he felt ashamed of last session, and Bente was not happy about any of the reactions she received when she told the group that she had been unfaithful to her husband'.

In the termination phase: 'We do not have much time left here now, and we have talked about how difficult it is for some of you to separate, and be on your own in the future without support from the others. This may contribute to strong reactions. We each take this differently and may be more or less sensitive to these changes: some may want to explore feelings that occur, while others may want to avoid such feelings, perhaps particularly those carrying sadness and loneliness'.

If patients arrive late for a session, the therapist will often not inform them about what took place earlier in the session, but focus on the group's reaction or lack of it. The meaning of the late arrival may be explored and interpreted when the session is running well. Often a latecomer may express something on behalf of the whole group.

If someone is absent, this patient is usually not contacted immediately after one absence, unless the therapist sees it necessary or worries strongly about the absence. (One time, a new patient was absent from the group, which worried me. I called him directly after the group session, and he told me he was preparing for hanging himself. After one hour on the phone, the immediate crisis was resolved, and the group therapy continued). Most often, I would wait until the next session and explore in the group the ideas about this absence and how the members felt. Even if the absence seems inevitable, the therapist should explore the patient's reactions to it on return, like 'How was it to be prevented from coming?' 'Did you think of the group when you were not here?' 'What reactions did you expect when you got back?'

If a patient is absent twice and there is no message, the therapist should try to make contact with that person by phone. The conversation should be short; the therapist should mention that the patient was missed and ask for the reasons for both the absence and maybe why the patient did not give any notice. I then usually say: 'I will see you in the next session'. If the patient is in doubt about returning, I usually assure him that he is not the only one with ambivalent feelings toward the group, and that it is important to come and discuss this in the group. If this is not helpful, I will express sympathy with the wish to terminate, but ask him to return in order to say goodbye. Only as a last resort, I may refer to the contract, or remind the patients that this way of acting is similar to some of the problems the patient initially presented as a central problem, i.e. give an interpretation.

When the patient returns to the group I will focus on the role the patient may have had in the group. Other patients are invited to identify with the patient and explore their own ambivalence and disappointment about the group, the therapist or other members, etc. They are also invited to explore their feelings towards the patient. I may then try to connect the patient's wish to quit with whatever may have happened and the developmental phase of the group.

In the working phase: 'I feel that it has not been so easy to be Arne lately. We are in the middle of a phase where everyone is expected to disclose the problematic ways of relating, which may have brought you here. Arne has been very open, and maybe that in itself is one of his problems. Even if many can identify with him, my feeling is that this has not been expressed clearly enough. The result has been that he has felt alone and let down by both the group and me.'

In the termination phase: 'I think Arne has been weighed down by the group during this last phase. He has told us about many episodes of loss in his life, and evidently these feelings are very strong and alive in him. Other group members may be more successful in shutting off these feelings, leaving it to him to do this job for many.' And one may add: 'For this reason it is great and also brave of him to return and explain how he was feeling, which perhaps has made it possible for others to get in touch with similar feelings, that often are mobilized by terminations and separations.'

### Example 2. Emotions are important

The therapist encourages the patients to express all kinds of feelings, especially those they feel discomfort at disclosing. In addition, the therapist names the non-verbalized feelings which are present in the room. Catharsis is considered to be therapeutic, but only if the feelings are integrated by exploring them and if it can be understood how they reflect the underlying conflicts. The therapist should pay special attention to the feelings that are *not* being expressed in the group:

'If I perceive the situation correctly, it seems as if the group is very sad today. It sounds as if Janet's perception of herself as boring and depreciated by everyone is some kind of echo of what several group members feel about themselves. I wonder if this feeling of "not having got enough" from parents is connected to the fact that we are approaching termination. As a matter of fact, we only have this session and another two, before we have to end.'

Affects may also have a defensive function for the group-as-a-whole, and are sometimes expressed by a single group member. Then the focus on the group-as-a-whole may be more important than on the one who expressed the feelings:

'There is a lot of irritation here today. Everything seems wrong and everyone seems to be somewhat discontent. First of all, I think that it is me you are dissatisfied with, but it seems less dangerous to fight amongst yourselves than criticizing me. Several of you opened up last session disclosing a lot of problems. I suppose many expected to get understanding and support. Instead I said something like "life can be difficult", which must have been perceived as rather indifferent.'

### Example 3. Acting out and jeopardizing the therapy

When patients start acting out non-verbalized affects or unconscious conflicts, my response will reflect my attempts at understanding, exploring and interpreting the behaviour. Since the same type of acting out on a behavioural level may represent different aspects of unconscious conflict, the therapist should scrutinize closer the leads he has got before interpreting. The maladaptive aspects of the acting out should always be included in the interpretation. Some possible formulations follow, which try to catch the essence in two patients who have been seeing each other outside the group ('pairing'):

'It seems that you want to take the intimacy you have felt for Eva in the group with you out in the world. Maybe you want to skip the difficulties you have had with getting close to other people. You may forget that the results of this may be that after a while you end up feeling like a stranger in the group, and in this way you may be lonely both inside and outside the group.'

Or: 'You seem to wish to express your feelings by doing things together instead of using words. I figure you are annoyed with me, since I demand that everything that goes on between you should take place here in the group, and that only words are permitted. You may not think of the fact that by neglecting to use what the group has to offer, you deprive yourself of the possibility of solving some of the central problems in your life.'

It is also possible to connect the incidence to the phase the group is in, and interpret it as an attempt to solve or avoid the tasks that the current stage represents. It is also possible to interpret on a group-as-a-whole level, if it seems plausible that a couple act out on behalf of the whole group.

### Example 4. Silence may function as a defence in a short-term group

The therapist's task is to understand the silence in the context of the here-and-now situation. If one or two patients are involved in silence over time, this also may be seen in the light of the group-as-a-whole.

'Maybe Einar represents the part of you all that wants the lid to be closed tight, fearing that you may be overwhelmed by all the pain and despair which is inside?'

Or: '. . . who would like to keep the lid on, fearing that if too much is let out, it would hurt or even damage others in the group?'

### Example 5. Dealing with sub-groups

'There seems to be a debate going on in the group between men and women, about whether we have a need for close intimate relationships or not. The women want and value such a relationship, while the men seem to think they can do well without. I think this debate represents a struggle or conflict that takes place within every one of you. Wanting to, but at the same time being scared by the prospect of having an intimate relationship. And, of course, as long as this debate goes on, on both these levels, the initiative to change can be postponed or avoided.'

### Example 6. Roles

When a patient seems to adapt to a special role in the group, the therapist may see this as a response to a need in the group, even though members are not put in roles by coincidence. Addressing this phenomenon is a commonly used tool in short-term groups. The therapist will try to understand, explore and interpret the function of this specific role in the group. Patients' roles typically have a protective and defensive function for the group. When the therapist interprets, he will start with describing the behaviour of the 'group delegate' and goes from there on to the group level. Sometimes the 'delegate' performs something the group wants from the therapist, and therefore the interpretation may often be tied up with a transference wish.

'The Professor': If 'the Professor' appears in the group, the therapist may think that the group needs reduction of anxiety by means of defence mechanisms like rationalizations and intellectualizing:

'It seems like you, Ivar, struggle with explaining all these difficult feelings. It is as if you believe that if you and the group understood "why", you would not find things so painful. I do not think you are alone in this, but that you represent the part of us all that wants to master and control painful and confusing feelings.'

'The Optimist': If the 'obsessional sprinkler of joy' appears in the group, the therapist understands that the group 'needs' praise and encouragement:

'Aina, you seem to be eager to comfort all the other members in the group. I think maybe several group members would have liked to get that support from me, the same way you wanted devotion and understanding from important persons earlier in your life. Could it be that you also think I am neglecting and hurting you the same way others in your life have done?'

'The Monopolizer': The patient who talks incessantly, monopolizing the time, may make the therapist understand that the group is very vulnerable and I might intervene in the following way:

'Jan, you seem very concerned about pulling the load for the group. I wonder if you in this way also protect others, who may feel relieved not having to talk about their own difficulties. They get off easier, and this may be why they let it happen.'

## How does the group react to interpretations?

When an interpretation is made it is important to pay attention to the group's reactions. Did the interpretation open things up for deeper communication and exploration, or did resistance and withdrawal increase? If the group opens up in an energetic further exploration of the theme, the interpretation was precise. If the group suddenly becomes silent and tense, the interpretation probably was close to target, but badly timed. The therapist may have to persevere and keep the group close to the focus, which was the basis for the interpretation.

# Part III

# Clinical research

Chapter 9

# Therapist adherence and competence

## Treatment fidelity

## Introduction

A treatment manual should contain a resumé of the theoretical background, treatment methods and an overview of interventions. It should also give clinical examples, indicating how to evaluate and to intervene. For research purposes it is also important to develop scales and measures to check if therapists do what they are supposed to do, and how competently they 'deliver' the therapies (Luborsky and Barber, 1993).

As clinicians we know that treatment should be individualized and tailor-made for each person. This may also be the ultimate ideal in treatments that are part of a clinical research project, but the design and formulation of research questions, and possibly treatment format, may require some standardization and modifications of regular treatment approaches. However, most psychodynamic psychotherapy manuals will seek to preserve the therapist's flexible position, and present principles and guideline for interventions, more than detailed prescriptions. This may be quite different from most manuals in cognitive behavioural approaches, which have a tendency of including more detailed instructions for procedure and interventions, and sometimes even offer a schedule for how therapy should proceed.

When the effectiveness of two or more different treatments is studied in a randomized clinical trial, a manual for each approach is needed, in order to effect that the patients receive approximately the same treatment, within each arm of the study.

## Developing scales

The main option of the SALT-GAP project is to study the significance of treatment duration. Accordingly, the two treatments we want to compare should be as similar as possible, so that differences in outcome may be attributed to the difference in treatment duration alone.

However, since we already have a lot of experience with short-term therapies, it would be unethical *not* to use this knowledge when a treatment manual is produced. Compared to longer-term therapies, the short-term therapies need some modifications in approach in the following respects: higher therapist activity, more circumscribed problem focus, more structure, more working in the here-and-now and more concern with termination.

The following questions have to be answered:

1. Are both therapies group analytic (psychodynamic)?
2. Is it possible to reliably distinguish between the short- term and long-term formats?
3. Are the therapies competently delivered and are there quality differences between short- and long-term therapy?

In order to answer these questions, two observers independently and blindly (without knowing whether the session was from STG or LTG) listened to and rated 40 group sessions. The sessions were randomly selected from a pool of 54 sessions, representative for all therapists.

The question of whether or not the therapies were psychodynamic was answered by consensus between the two evaluators. Their evaluation was based on the presence of work with transference and resistances on group and individual levels, that the groups were process oriented and whether therapist and group members worked with interpersonal issues.

In order to check the possibility to reliably differentiate between short-term and long-term therapies, we developed a measure with 20 items based on therapy differences emphasized in the treatment manuals, covering the dimensions of therapist activity, interventions, focus and process. The items were rated on a scale from 0 (not at all) to 4 (very much). When we excluded items with a low interrater reliability (intraclass correlation coefficient < 0.65), we ended up with the following items: level of therapist activity, degree of circumscribed focus, work in the here-and-now and work with termination. We found that patients in STG had significantly more work done on circumscribed problems and worked significantly more in the here-and-now, as suggested in the treatment manuals. Thus we were able to distinguish between the two forms of therapy. Level of therapist activity, however, was equal in the two groups.

We developed a therapist competence measure with eight items that were rated on the same scale, from 0 (low) to 4 (very high). Therapist competence turned out to be equal in both formats, ranging from moderate to high (STG = 2.7, SD 0.5, range 1.7–3.4; LTG = 2.3, SD 0.5, range 1.9–3.1). We have previously reported that there were no significant differences in therapeutic alliance or group cohesion (at sessions 3, 10 and 17) in the two group formats, which at least indicates that the two different therapies consistently represent a similar impact on group members (Bakali et al., 2010). The interrater reliability coefficient on all process and competence ratings ranged from 0.70 to 0.94. Thus, we can conclude this section stating that the therapies were both psychodynamic, the two formats could be distinguished from each other and the therapies were delivered with the same competence in STG and LTG.

## The adherence and competence scales

All items are rated on a scale from 0 = not at all to 4 = very much.
   Therapy adherence:

a.   Therapist activity, global   . . . . . .
b.   Signs of prepared (circumscribed) focus

    i.   Patients say what they are going to work with.
    ii.   The therapist asks patients or reminds them, what they are going to work with.
    iii.   One or more patients are focused on interpersonal problems.
    iv.   The patient refers to discussions with the therapist about focus in the preparation (individual) sessions.
    v.   Patients ask fellow group members about the focus for their treatment.

Mean score (i.–v.)   . . . . . .

c.   Working in the here-and-now   . . . . . .
d.   Work on termination   . . . . . .

Therapist competence:

1.   Global impression of the quality of therapist's work (interpersonal skills). Rate each sub-item separately:

    1.1   The therapist seems to be aware of individual patients as well as the group-as-a-whole (seems to recognize both elements)   . . . . . .
    1.2   The therapist responds to the patients in an accepting and understanding manner   . . . . . .
    1.3   The therapist shows evidence of listening receptively   . . . . . .
    1.4   The therapist attempts to maintain a focused line of inquiry through questions, clarifications and sometimes confrontations   . . . . . .
    1.5   The therapist shows evidence of warmth and empathy towards patients   . . . . . .
    1.6   The therapist avoids blaming the patient or the group   . . . . . .
    1.7   The therapist seems flexible and tuned to the patients' and the group's needs   . . . . . .
    1.8   The therapist avoids complex, unclear and overly long interventions   . . . . . .

# Chapter 10

# Experiences and challenges in implementing the project

## General

The SALT-GAP (short- and long-term group analytic psychotherapy) project intended to address several areas of concern in contemporary group psychotherapy research. There has been a neglect of systematic small- and large-scale research studies, which has resulted in a scarce evidence base for the efficacy/effectiveness of psychodynamic therapies. Consequently there are too few high quality (randomized clinical trials) studies done, which is the gold standard in psychotherapy outcome research. There are also very few systematic studies of long-term group psychotherapy (group analysis), even though long-term groups are quite common in clinical practice.

Our research project, including this book, should be seen in the light of an increasing demand for evidence-based practice, which we have experienced in the field of psychiatry and mental health services during the last two decades. The purpose is to secure that the health-care interventions given to the population are according to the best available knowledge in the field. Another side of the coin covers economic considerations. Given the high costs of health services, it is important that the assistance given has demonstrated efficacy/effectiveness in systematic high quality studies. The quality of research evidence is accordingly ordered in a hierarchy with reviews of randomized controlled trials (RCTs) on the top, in descending order followed by at least one RCT, other controlled studies, observational (naturalistic) studies, and with expert judgement and clinical wisdom on the bottom of the scale. The health authorities and professional organizations in the UK and the USA have been central agents in promoting these ideas. The consequences for the psychotherapy field have been mixed. On one hand, therapy approaches that more readily can be operationalized according to the standards required by randomized clinical trials (RCT), like CBT (cognitive behavioural therapy) and IPT (interpersonal therapy), have been favoured, since more research evidence for efficacy exists. At the same time, therapies with less research evidence, like psychodynamic therapies, may be considered to be not only less researched, but less effective. A more recent development is a growing acknowledgement of the importance of 'clinical wisdom', cultural context and patient preferences, in an effective clinical practice (APA, 2006). Positive consequences from the 'evidenced

practice debate' have been that these standards have created lively debates in
the field about what valid research methodology is, and they have also represented an impetus to start and implement more psychotherapy research, also in
psychodynamic psychotherapy. There has been much concern that systematic
research on clinical samples may impinge destructively on the treatment, and
that RCT requirements, like for example training of therapists according to
treatment manuals or homogeneity of patient diagnosis across study samples,
give results that readily cannot be generalized back to a regular clinical situation. There has also been a deep worry that third-party payers and health
authorities would uncritically ignore clinical wisdom and support the use of
shorter and cheaper therapies, only because it might reduce costs.

My view, which I think is shared by many fellow clinicians and researchers, is
that most evidence indicates that the mental health field needs several forms of
psychotherapeutic approaches. No single theoretical approach has so far demonstrated a general superiority in effect in comparison to several other therapies.

With this contextual background, I would now like to present some of the
experiences we had and challenges we met during the implementation of this
project. These will be described from the view of the project leader who had
to sell the project to health authorities, hospital administrators and group
therapists, in order to obtain funding and recruit therapists who were
interested in and permitted to engage in clinical research that was administered
from the outside. Just as important is to what degree therapists could be
persuaded to introduce more systematic research into their everyday clinical
work, to revise treatment approaches and submit to rules dictated by the
research design and methodology. And how did they feel about that?

Our experiences may be of help for others who would want to implement
similar projects. However, each research project will be shaped by the immi-
nent research questions, chosen design and methodology, and not least the
funding, which entails that everyone who undertakes such a project will have
to meet new challenges and find their own solutions.

Foremost, a successful implementation of small- or large-scale studies
depends on the possibility to build a network including both competent
researchers and clinicians, who are bold and motivated enough to carry out
the work. I use bold, since it really requires courage to start out to do a
systematic evaluation of your own psychotherapeutic enterprise, not least
because being a psychotherapist often involves a lifelong commitment which
is highly personal and strongly tied up with our identity. Thus, there will
naturally be some apprehension when others (researchers) are invited in to put
the spotlight on and evaluate parts of this activity.

## Planners' view

The basic prerequisites for carrying through a clinical research project are
naturally relevant research questions and ideas of how they can be studied,
and time and money to be able to create an opportunity to do so. You also

need a strong interest and enthusiasm about the project, both personally and in your coworkers.

The ideas of this project followed from my doctoral thesis which consisted of studying outcome and process in an observational study of long-term analytic groups with outpatients (Lorentzen, 2003). While I worked on that, I had been struck by the paradox that while a majority of clinical groups, at least in Europe, seemed to be of a long-term format, research had almost exclusively been carried out on short-term groups. Also, the lack of research on psychodynamic groups was striking.

It was easy to establish a steering group for the project and two colleagues with interest and experience in psychotherapy research were included. We were fortunate to quickly obtain a grant over three years, from the regional health authorities. A newly acquired university position on my part offered a welcome opportunity for doing research.

We needed several study sites in order to recruit enough therapists and patients, and we went out nation wide with a project description and an invitation to participate. The letter was addressed to the administrators of outpatient clinics and to private practitioners. A main argument for the project was that it could flexibly be made part of the regular clinical work in the clinic. We offered initial training and yearly seminars for participants, plus regular supervision in the treatment phase. We also announced the project in professional circles, in order to recruit therapists. Initially we felt a little disappointed because of 'little' response. In retrospect, however, we are very happy that we ended up with 'only' three sites, comprising five outpatient clinics and two private practitioners, which again represented nine experienced therapists who were interested and strongly motivated to participate. The size of the network and the workload has been about what our small, low budget project could handle.

We then started a series of seminars for the therapists with the following tasks:

a.  Discuss the practical implementation of the research and integration of the groups in the clinical reality in their workplace.
b.  Agree on design, research instruments, procedures etc.
c.  Discuss and accept the treatment manuals.
d.  Training in delivering manualized treatments.
e.  Negotiate written contracts.

We also had seminars for research coordinators about structured diagnostic interviews, psychodynamic interviews, interviews for evaluation of quality of object relations, etc. As part of this training we also carried out several ratings and interrater reliability checks. Procedures and time-points for data collection and transportation of data were decided and contracts written.

### *What were the main challenges?*

In the steering group we had previously experienced that it was possible to integrate the therapist and researcher role in a fruitful way, mainly in private practice (Lorentzen, 2003). This made it easier to argue for the present project and the necessary adjustments in routines. However, many negotiations were needed and modifications on both sides were necessary. Some requirements, like that of randomization or that the therapists should not be able to refuse to take some patients on, we were not willing to change. During these negotiations we felt some concern that potential therapists would drop out, but this apprehension soon waned after some preliminary meetings, as we felt that the therapists became increasingly committed.

The main motivational challenges both initially and throughout the project were centred around the fear of 'contaminating' the clinical situation, which, of course, sometimes is a realistic worry. Most often, however, I suspect that many therapists project their own apprehension about being 'researched' onto the patients, who in my experience often find it interesting to be part of a research project. It is easy to understand why most clinicians find it challenging to have their practice scrutinized, and we have a tradition for pushing the patients to the front. On the other hand, researchers may in heated discussions question most clinical 'truths', which at times may be quite provoking for a clinician who feels that his or her therapies, by and large, are running well.

We knew most of the therapists from other professional situations before we started our cooperation, which was helpful in the work, and I think that an initial trust grew as we discussed the different aspects of the project, including treatment manuals.

If we thought that the clinicians were too protective of the clinical situation, we would argue in favour of more research, based on the facts that as many as five to forty per cent of patients regularly dropped out of group therapy, that many patients did not respond to the treatment in spite of substantial investment on both sides (e.g. Lorentzen *et al.*, 2011) and that some patients deteriorate (five to ten per cent; Callahan and Hynan, 2005; Lambert and Ogles, 2004) during our treatment. We highlighted findings like this as a professional rationale and ethical justification for doing clinical research.

## Clinicians' view
(Horneland *et al.*, 2012)

The clinicians have in retrospect reported that it was easy to agree to participate in the project, since the design seemed to be adapted to the regular way of handling referrals. Also, the inclusion/exclusion criteria seemed to favour those patients who usually would be included in the groups.

Many felt inspired when they could contribute to increased knowledge about selection criteria for groups. They also found pleasure in meeting colleagues working in the same area. The fact that the project was seen as important made many proud of being a part of it. The groups were just as diverse and unpredictable as regular clinical groups, but some challenges existed, since some aspects differentiated these groups from regular clinical practice:

1. The patients in these groups had been randomized and could not themselves choose treatment length. This may have caused some premature terminations or a wish to continue the treatment after the short-term groups.
2. The therapists had to accept 'ready made' groups, and missed the usual possibility for evaluating patients and composing their own groups. Subsequently, they would sometimes perceive an unbalance between individual and group needs. Some inclusions seemed questionable, but still the therapists were not allowed to take anyone out of the group. Having a group member with 'questionable suitability' may prematurely have 'scared' other patients out of the group.
3. The number of sessions was fixed, and sometimes group members remained in the groups even though they only had insignificant problems, while some terminated 'prematurely', and both solutions may have affected the groups negatively.
4. Audio recording of some sessions seemed to be accepted by all, but created some apprehension in patients and therapist initially.
5. Repeated ratings of evaluation forms by the patients, which were collected by the therapists, and irregularities to do so on the part of the patients, were to be treated dynamically, like any other form of acting out. Many patients found the forms interesting and clinically relevant, while some felt it was an unwanted burden.
6. Some therapists found it hard to urge the patients not to start any new treatment during the first year after termination of the group.

After all data was collected, and all treatments terminated, as many as ninety per cent of the patients were willing to come for a three year follow-up, and I think this demonstrates that we as clinicians and researchers have succeeded fairly well in our combined endeavours.

# Chapter 11

# Some preliminary results

As a conclusion of this manual, a few results from the study are presented, as examples of how clinically relevant evidence can be brought forth. The data analysis in this project is ongoing and the findings can loosely be categorized as (a) outcome of treatment, (b) group process factors and (c) mechanisms of change.

## Outcome

We found that the typical patient in the whole group had a significant change in symptoms and psychosocial functioning across the three-year study period, but there was not a significant difference in change for the average patient in STG compared to LTG.

However, when we compared patients with and without personality disorder in the two groups, the picture changed. Patients who had a personality disorder had an equal change during the first six months (during the short-term therapy) in the two groups, but they changed significantly more in LTG from six to 36 months. Patients without a personality disorder had a larger change during the first six months. From six to 36 months, patients in LTG changed more, but they never quite caught up with the STG patients, concerning improvement in symptoms.

The clinical implications of this are that patients should be closely evaluated for the presence of personality disorder before treatment length is decided. This may save everyone involved from destructive ruptures in therapeutic alliance and attachment to other group members. It can also save patients without personality disorder from going longer in therapy than is necessary. In both cases, human and economic savings will be the result.

We also calculated how many patients had a *clinically* significant change across three years. A clinically significant change means that the patient both improves significantly and that he moves into the range of the normal population. It turned out that a significantly higher number of the patients with personality disorders had a clinically significant change in the LTG, than in STG. Around five per cent of the patients deteriorated when the outcome was averaged across the four main outcome measures. Also there was no difference in number of deteriorators between patients in STG and LTG.

## Group processes

Group cohesion has long been established as an important therapeutic factor in groups, sometimes compared to the therapeutic alliance of individual therapy. A large number of studies have demonstrated a relationship between early cohesion and outcome of group therapy. An important problem, however, has been that too many measures have been in use, and the result is that the cohesion–outcome relationship has varied between measures, as well as who the evaluator has been. Johnson and colleagues (2005) demonstrated, by carrying out several explorative and confirmative factor analyses of items from four commonly used group relationship measures (empathy, therapeutic alliance, cohesion and group climate) encompassing 662 patients and 111 groups, that cohesion in groups consists of structural as well as relational factors (qualitative). We have in our study replicated and expanded these findings (Bakali et al., 2009). The qualitative factors consist of three independent factors: positive bonding and work relationships, as well as a negative factor (avoidance and conflict). The structural components (horizontal and vertical) are member–member, member–therapist and member–group relationships. We found that the member–therapist alliance was most important early in therapy, while the member–member relationship was more important later in therapy. Our study indicates that a greater focus on the individual therapy goal(s) as well as the therapeutic tasks they imply, would improve therapy, as would a stronger focus on the member–therapist relationship.

## Change mechanisms

We have so far analyzed few of these, but we have studied the patients' negative attributional style. To measure this, patients in both STG and LTG completed an Attributional Style Questionnaire (ASQ; Petersen et al., 1982) every six months across two years. The questionnaire is composed of 12 (imagined) events, half of which put the patient in a positive light and a half that describe the outcome for the patient negatively. Six items cover affiliation and six cover achievement. One example of achievement is: 'You have been looking for a new job unsuccessfully for some time', and of affiliation: 'You meet a friend who acts hostilely towards you'. The patient is then asked how this may be explained (on a scale from 1 = 'totally due to the other person or a coincidence' to 7 = 'totally due to me'). The same scale is also used to rate how stable (across time) this pattern is and how global (extensive) it is. The sum score on the six bad events is a measure of the patient's tendency of being self-critical and self-blaming and to have a pessimistic outlook referring to most future accomplishments and relationships. We found a significantly larger reduction of this tendency in LTG patients across two years, which turned out to explain some of the increased improvement in interpersonal problems in LTG as compared to STG. This points to 'change in negative attributional style' as a probable mechanism of change in LTG.

Clinically, therapists should be alert to signs of negative attribution in patients, especially if they devaluate their own *positive* achievements or have a tendency of unilaterally criticizing and blaming themselves when interpersonal conflicts take place. The persistence and pervasiveness of such attitudes should be challenged by the therapist. ASQ was originally developed to measure 'learned helplessness' and change in depressives receiving CBT.

Another possible mechanism of change to be studied in this project is potential change in *self-understanding* (Connolly *et al.*, 1999).

## Publications in the study

Bakali, J. V., Baldwin, S. A., and Lorentzen, S. (2009). Modeling group process constructs at three stages in group psychotherapy. *Psychotherapy Research*, 19(3), 332–343.

Bakali, J. V., Wilberg, T., Hagtvet, K. A., and Lorentzen, S. (2010). Sources accounting for alliance and cohesion at three stages in group psychotherapy. Variance component analyses. *Group Dynamics: Theory, Research, and Practice*, 14(4), 368–383.

Bakali, J. V., Wilberg, T., Klungsøyr, J., and Lorentzen, S. (in press). Development of group climate in short- and long-term psychodynamic group psychotherapy. *International Journal of Group Psychotherapy*.

Lorentzen, S., Bakali, J. V., Hersoug, A. G., Hagtvet, K. A., Ruud, T., and Høglend, P. (2011). Impact of group length and therapist professional characteristics on development of therapeutic alliance. *Clinical Psychology and Psychotherapy*. DOI: 10.1002/cpp.758.

Lorentzen, S. (2012). Writing manuals for psychodynamic group treatments. *Group Analysis*, 45(1), 28–45.

Lorentzen, S., Ruud, T., Fjeldstad, A. and Høglend, P. (in press) Comparing short- and long-term dynamic psychotherapy: A randomised clinical trial. *British Journal of Psychiatry*.

Horneland, M., Børnes Sande, D., Høbye, K., Knutsen, H., and Lorentzen, S. (2012). Can the clinician–researcher gap be bridged? Experiences from a randomized clinical trial in analytic/dynamic group psychotherapy. *Group Analysis*, 45(1), 84–98.

Skjøstad, K. (2011). Den som leter, finner ikke. Den som ikke leter, blir oppsøkt. En drøfting av motstandsfenomener i gruppeterapi, sett i sammenheng med administrative forhold som påvirker deltakeres opplevelse av valgfrihet. *Matrix*, 28(1), 48–66.

# Appendix

## Overview of diagnostic interviews and measures in SALT-GAP

Diagnosis:

- Diagnostic and Statistical Manual (DSM-IV; American Psychiatric Association, 1994).

  o  Axis I: Symptomatic reaction.
  o  Axis II: Personality disorder.
  o  Axis V: GAF (Global Assessment of Functioning).

- DSM-IV diagnoses axes I and II were obtained with the use of semistructured interviews: We used MINIPLUS (Sheehan et al., 2002) for Axis I and SCID-II (First et al., 1997) for Axis II.
- Global Assessment of Functioning (GAF) (Axis V). We used a version split on symptoms and functioning, and they were rated through a separate interview (Goldman et al., 1992).
- Quality of Object Relationships (QOR) was also rated through a semistructured interview (Høglend et al., 2006).

Primary outcome measures:

- Symptom Check List (SCL-90-R; Derogatis, 1977). Ninety questions covering all possible symptoms. Gives an index plus scores on ten dimensions. Self rating.
- Inventory of Interpersonal Problems (IIP-64; Alden et al., 1990). Sixty-four questions that give an index for degree of interpersonal problems and a profile with eight personality variables on a circumplex. Self rating.
- Global Assessment of Functioning, split version (GAF-Symptom and GAF-Functioning; Goldman et al., 1992). Rated by an external evaluator.

Secondary outcome measures:

- Clinical Global Impression (CGI; Guy, 1976). Likert scale. Eight-step scale. Scored by therapist and patients.
- Target complaints. Operationalization of central subjective problems, rated on 12-step scale (Battle et al., 1966).
- Structural Analysis of Social Behavior (SASB; Benjamin, 1988, 1996).

Process measures:

- Working Alliance Inventory (Tracey and Kokotovic, 1989).
- Cohesion (Lese and MacNair-Semands, 2000).
- Group Climate Questionnaire (GCQ; MacKenzie, 1981).
- Audio recordings (Treatment adherence and therapist competence; Scales, see below).

Change mechanisms:

- Attributional Style Questionnaire (ASQ; Petersen et al., 1982).
- Self-Understanding of Interpersonal Patterns (SUIP; Connolly et al., 1999).

# Bibliography

Alden, L. E., Wiggins, J. S., and Pincus, A. L. (1990). Construction of circumplex scales from the Inventory of Interpersonal Problems. *Journal of Personality Assessment*, 55, 521–536.

American Psychiatric Association. (1994). *Diagnostic and Statistical Manual of Mental Disorders (DSM-IV)*. Washington, DC: Author.

Bakali, J. V., Baldwin, S. A., and Lorentzen, S. (2009). Modeling group process constructs at three stages in group psychotherapy. *Psychotherapy Research*, 19(3), 332–343.

Bakali, J. V., Wilberg, T., Hagtvet, K. A., and Lorentzen, S. (2010). Sources accounting for alliance and cohesion at three stages in group psychotherapy. Variance component analyses. *Group Dynamics: Theory, Research, and Practice*, 14(4), 368–383.

Bateman, A. and Fonagy, P. (2009). Randomized controlled trial of outpatient mentalization-based treatment versus structured clinical management for borderline personality disorders. *American Journal of Psychiatry*, 166,1355–1364.

Battle, C., Imber, S., Hoehn-Saric, R., Stone, A. R., Nash, E. H., and Frank, J. D. (1966). Target complaints as criteria of improvement. *American Journal of Psychotherapy*, 20, 184–192.

Benjamin, L. S. (1988). *SASB Short Form User's Manual*. Salt Lake City, Utah: Intrex Interpersonal Institute Inc.

Benjamin, L. S. (1996). A clinician-friendly version of the Interpersonal Circumplex: Structural Analysis of Social Behavior (SASB). *Journal of Personality Assessment*, 66, 248–266.

Bernard, H., Burlingame, G., Flores, P., Greene, L., Joyce, A., Kobos, J. C., Feirman, D. (2008). Clinical practice guidelines for group psychotherapy. *International Journal of Group Psychotherapy*, 58(4), 455–542.

Bion W. R. (1974). *Experiences in Groups and Other Papers*. London: Tavistock Publications.

Burlingame, G. M., Fuhriman, A., and Mosier, J. (2003). The differential effectiveness of group psychotherapy: A meta-analytic perspective. *Group Dynamics: Theory, Research, and Practice*, 7, 3–12.

Burlingame, G. M., MacKenzie, K. R. and Strauss, B. (2004). Small-group treatment: Evidence for effectiveness and mechanisms of change. In M. J. Lambert (Ed.), *Bergin and Garfield's Handbook of Psychotherapy and Behavior Change* (pp. 647–696). New York: John Wiley.

Burlingame, G. M., Strauss, B., and Joyce, A. S. Clinical mechanisms and effectiveness of small-group treatment. In M. J. Lambert (Ed.), *Bergin and Garfield's Handbook of Psychotherapy and Behavior Change*. In press.

Callahan, J. L., and Hynan, M. T. (2005). Models of psychotherapy outcome: Are they applicable in training clinics? *Psychological Services*, 2, 65–69.

Centre for Psychological Services Research, School of Health and Related Research; University of Sheffield, UK. (2009). A systematic review of the efficacy and clinical effectiveness of group analysis analytic/dynamic group psychotherapy. Available at: http://www.groupanalysis.org/uploadedfiles/workshops/IGA_GAS_FINAL_REPORT_UPDATED.pdf

Connolly, M. B., Crits-Christoph, P., Shelton, R. C., Hollon, S., Kurtz, J., and Barber, J. P. (1999). The reliability and validity of a measure of self-understanding of interpersonal patterns. *Journal of Counseling Psychology*, 4, 472–482.

De Maré, P. B. (1972). *Perspectives in Group Psychotherapy*. London: Allen and Unwin.

Derogatis, L. H. (1977). *The SCL-90-R: Administration, Scoring and Procedures. Manual I*. Baltimore, MD: Clinical Psychometric Research Unit, John Hopkins University School of Medicine.

First, M. B, Gibbon, M., Spitzer, R. L., Williams. J. B., and Benjamin, L. S. (1997). *User's Guide for the DSM-IV Personality Disorders*. Washington, DC: American Psychiatric Press.

Foulkes, S. H. (1977). *Therapeutic Group Analysis* (second printing). New York: International Universities Press.

Foulkes, S. H., and Anthony, E. J. (1984). *Group Psychotherapy. The Psychoanalytical Approach*. London: Maresfield Reprints.

Fuhriman, A. and Burlingame, G. M. (1994). Group psychotherapy: Research and practice. In A. Fuhriman and G. M. Burlingame (Eds.) *Handbook of Group Psychotherapy. An Empirical and Clinical Synthesis* (pp. 3–40). New York, John Wiley.

Goldman, H. H., Skodol, A. E., and Lave, T. R. (1992). Revising axis V for DSM-IV: a review of measures of social functioning. *American Journal of Psychiatry*, 149(9), 1148–1156.

Guy, W. (1976). *ECDEU Assessment Manual for Psychopharmacology*. Rev. Rockville, MD: U.S. National Institute of Health, Psychopharmacology Research Branch.

Høglend, P., Amlo, S., Marble, A., Bøgwald, K-P., Sørbye, Ø., Sjaastad, M. C., and Heyerdahl, O. (2006). Analysis of the patient-therapist relationship in dynamic psychotherapy: an experimental study of transference interpretations. *American Journal of Psychiatry*, 163, 1739–1746.

Horneland, M., Børnes Sande, D., Høbye, K., Knutsen, H., and Lorentzen, S. (2012). Can the clinician-researcher gap be bridged? Experiences from a randomized clinical trial in analytic/dynamic group psychotherapy. *Group Analysis*, 45(1), 84–98.

Johnson, J. E., Burlingame, G. M., Olsen, J. A., Davies, D. R., and Gleave, R. L. (2005). Group climate, cohesion, alliance, and empathy in group psychotherapy: Multilevel structural equation models. *Journal of Counseling Psychology*, 52(3), 310–321.

Lambert, M. J. and Ogles, B. M. (2004). The efficacy and effectiveness of psychotherapy. In M. J. Lambert (Ed.), *Bergin and Garfield's Handbook of Psychotherapy and Behavior Change* (pp. 139–193). New York: Wiley.

Lau, M. and Kristensen, E. (2007). Outcome of systemic and analytic group psychotherapy for adult women with history of intrafamilial childhood sexual abuse: A randomized controlled study. *Acta Psychiatrica Scandinavica*, 116(2), 96–104.

Lese, K. P. and MacNair-Semands, R. R. (2000). The Therapeutic Factors Inventory: development of a scale. *Group*, 24(4), 303–317.

Lorentzen, S. (2003). Long-term analytic group psychotherapy with out-patients. Evaluation of process and change. Doctoral thesis. Faculty of Medicine, University of Oslo, Norway.

Lorentzen, S., Bøgwald, K-P., and Høglend, P. (2002). Change during and after long-term analytic group psychotherapy. *International Journal of Group Psychotherapy*, 52, 419–429.

Lorentzen, S., Høglend, P., Martinsen, E. W., and Ringdal, E. (2011). Practice-based evidence: Patients who did not respond to Group Analysis. *International Journal of Group Psychotherapy*, 61(3), 367–395.

Luborsky, L. and Barber, J. P. (1993). Benefits of adherence to psychotherapy manuals, and where to get them. In N. E. Miller, L. Luborsky and J. P. Docherty (Eds.), *Psychodynamic Treatment Research: A Handbook for Clinical Practice* (pp. 211–226). New York: Basic Books.

Lundqvist, G., Svedin, C. G., Hansson, K., and Broman, I. (2006). Group therapy for women sexually abused as children: Mental health before and after group therapy. *Journal of Interpersonal Violence*, 21(12), 1665–1677.

MacKenzie, K. R. (1981). Measurement of group climate. *Journal of Group Psychotherapy*, 31, 287–296.

MacKenzie, K. R. (1997). *Time-Managed Group Psychotherapy: Effective Clinical Applications*. Washington, DC: American Psychiatric Association.

Malan, D. H., Balfour, F. H., Hood, V. G., and Shooter, A. M. (1976). Group psychotherapy. A long-term follow-up study. *Archives of General Psychiatry*, 33, 1303–1315.

Orlinsky, D. E., Grawe, K., and Parks, B. K. (2004). Evaluating the ingredients of therapeutic efficacy. In A. E. Bergin and S. L. Garfield (Eds.), *Handbook of Psychotherapy and Behavior Change* (pp. 270–376). New York: John Wiley.

Petersen, C., Semmel, A., von Baeyer, C., Abrahamson, L. Y., Metalsky, G. I., and Seligman, M. E. P. (1982). The attributional style questionnaire. *Cognitive Therapy and Research*, 6(3), 287–300.

Pines, M. (Ed.) (1983). *The Evolution of Group Analysis*. London: Routledge and Kegan Paul.

Roberts, J. (2000). Interventions. In D. Kennard, J. Roberts, and D. A. Winther (Eds.), *A Work Book of Group-Analytic Interventions* (pp. 2–11). London and Philadelphia: Jessica Kingsley Publishers.

Sheehan, D., Janavs, J., Baker, R., Harnett-Sheehan, K., Knapp, E., and Sheehan, M. (2002). *Mini International Neuropsychiatric Interview*. Tampa: University of South Florida Press.

Spiegel, D., and Classen, C. (2000). *Group Therapy for Cancer Patients*. New York: Basic Books.

Tracey, T. J. and Kokotovic, A. M. (1989). Factor structure of the Working Alliance Inventory. *Psychological Assessment: A Journal of Consulting and Clinical Psychology*, 1(3), 207–210.

Waltz, J., Addis, M. E., Koerner, K., and Jacobsen, N. S. (1993). Testing the integrity of a psychotherapy protocol: Assessment of adherence and competence. *Journal of Consulting and Clinical Psychology*, 61, 620–630.

Yalom, I. D. and Leszcz, M. (2005). *The Theory and Practice of Group Psychotherapy*. New York: Basic Books.

# Index

For Product Safety Concerns and Information please contact our EU
representative  GPSR@taylorandfrancis.com
Taylor & Francis Verlag GmbH, Kaufingerstraße 24, 80331 München, Germany

www.ingramcontent.com/pod-product-compliance
Lightning Source LLC
Chambersburg PA
CBHW070351270326
41926CB00017B/4083